Essex
GIRLS

Essex
GIRLS

KAREN BOWMAN

AMBERLEY

For my own Essex Girls, Rachel & Alexes, and my Essex Lad, Tom.

First published 2010

Amberley Publishing Plc
Cirencester Road, Chalford,
Stroud, Gloucestershire, GL6 8PE

www.amberley-books.com

British Library Cataloguing in Publication Data.
A catalogue record for this book is available from the British Library.

ISBN 978 1 84868 895 7

Typeset in 10pt on 12pt Sabon.
Typesetting and Origination by FONTHILLDESIGN.
Printed in the UK.

CONTENTS

ACKNOWLEDGEMENTS

Illustrations in this book are reproduced by kind permission of the following: Robert Bowman; The Cromwell Museum; Essex Record Office; Midge Frazel; Robert Hallmann; The National Portrait Gallery; and Bob Nicholls. Other illustrations are from the author's own collection.

Thanks also to Linda Rhodes of Barking Library Local Studies Centre; Jennie Butler and the staff at the Essex Record Office; Matthew Bailey of the National Portrait Gallery; John Goldsmith of the Cromwell Museum Huntingdon; the National Archives; Val Jackson for introducing me to Edith Swan-Neck; Ben Joscelyne of The Josselin Society; and Claire Harvey (née Joscelyne) for kindly allowing me to reproduce a part of her family history. Thanks also to my family for their support in this venture.

A very special thanks goes to Robert Hallmann for his wonderful Essex photography and invaluable advice.

INTRODUCTION

Women's rights and status have changed over the centuries, not always for the better. With equality for women built into the law today, it's easy to overlook the lack of rights our forebears suffered. To better understand the achievements and/or notoriety of women throughout history, it is first necessary to understand the constraints that were placed upon them.

From birth, women were taught that they were inferior to men. Shaped by the Church, Medieval and Renaissance society led women to believe they were instruments of the devil, the only imperfection in God's Creation. Strong stuff by today's standards, but very real in 1558 when John Knox, in his treatise, *The First Blast of the Trumpet against the Monstrous Regiment of Women*, wrote 'Woman in her greatest perfection was made to serve and obey man'.

Young girls were hardly given any freedom; they were raised to obey their parents without question, marry, and bear children. When they did embark upon matrimony they were expected to 'render unquestioning obedience to their husband and to learn in silence from him in all subjection'.

Education provided little escape. A waste of time to all but the rich, it was thought to corrupt; where it did occur, its purpose was to produce a good and moral wife, not to promote independent thinking. When exceptions arose, public opinion was still reserved; for example, Lady Jane Grey was quite a scholar 'for a woman', and both Catherine of Aragon and Katherine Parr, wives of Henry VIII, were judged 'virtuous despite their education'.

For women, sex before marriage was forbidden, and sex within it was deemed by the Church only for 'the procreation of children'. Even the service used to marry a couple required the bride to vow to be 'bonaire and buxom in bed and board'. Pregnancy was usually an annual event, many women dying in childbirth. It was not unusual for an expectant mother to not only prepare for her confinement, but also make arrangements for someone to care for the child should she die.

With a woman's body and her goods becoming her husband's property when she married, and the law allowing him to do whatever he wanted with them, it is needless to say that infidelity in a wife was not tolerated. An adulterous wife of a peer could be executed if the king granted her husband's petition. Also, a wife who killed her husband was guilty of petty treason and not murder, the punishment being death by burning.

Thus, throughout history, a wife who displeased her husband in any way, real or imagined, could be turned out of the house with just a shift to cover her, and no right of redress. Divorces were rare and annulments were granted only by an ecclesiastical court or by the Pope.

The Anglo-Saxon woman, however, enjoyed more legal rights than her subsequent sisters, Norman or otherwise. Within marriage, all finances and property were held jointly with her husband, except for the *Morgengifu*. This 'morning gift' was as an essential part of all wedding arrangements, which a prospective husband was required to pay to the woman herself. One wealthy Saxon, Godwine of the early eleventh century, promised his future wife a pound's weight in gold, an estate, 150 acres at Burmarsh, thirty oxen, twenty cows, ten horses, and ten slaves. Wives, in turn, had control over the *Morgengifu*; they were at liberty to give it away, sell it, or bequeath it as they pleased. The marriage contract also required the husband to promise that he would properly maintain his future wife, and state what inheritance he would leave her should he die. Additionally, the woman remained under the protection of her kin even after marriage. This meant that, even if she moved away from them after the marriage, her kin could still help her if she became embroiled in legal difficulties. Married women, it appears, had some power.

This legal recognition of the woman within marriage all but ended with the Norman Conquest. By changing the laws of kinship, the Normans created the concept of the 'chattel wife', which endured until the end of the nineteenth century, effectively denying a woman rights over her estate and her children. After the conquest, only an unmarried woman of property shared a legal ability to make a will and sign documents. She forfeited these rights when she married. On the death of her husband, she was entitled to one third of his land upon which to support herself. Widowhood became a desirable condition. As a widow, a woman again became the head of the household and, herself, a valuable commodity. If a man could convince a widow to marry him he could increase his and his family's power and wealth. Many chose to remain widows, a reasonable choice under the circumstances, or they became nuns.

1

WOMEN OF PROPERTY, POWER, PRESTIGE AND PIETY

NUNS OF BARKING ABBEY

At that time when Sebbi ... ruled the east Saxons, Theodore appointed over them Earconwald to be their bishop ... before he was made bishop (he) builded two goodley monasteries, one for himself the other for his sister Ethelburga ... in the province of the East Saxons at the place that is named in Bericingum.

A t a time when women were not allowed to serve as reeves, mayors, or go to Parliament, the Abbesses of Barking were amongst the most powerful and independent women in Essex. From the Dark Ages until the Dissolution of the Monasteries, the nuns of Barking Abbey held the office of 'baron ex-officio', supplying the king with 'thirteen knight's fees and a half', (the fees to pay men to fight for the king) and had precedence over all other abbesses. Though little is known about the lives of the ordinary women who dedicated themselves to St Benedict, becoming members of one of the richest institutions in England, they were still inextricably linked to the story of the abbey itself.

At a time of devastating plague, Erkenwald, Bishop of London, founded two abbeys in AD 666, one for himself and one for his sister, Ethelburga. Bericingum (Barking) was to be Ethelburga's domain. Dedicated to St Mary, the abbey was endowed by the Christian East Saxon princes; before long the abbey's land and properties stretched between the river Roding and the Dagenham Beam river as far as the Thames to the south and the 'great forest' to the north. These lands eventually became the manor of Barking, the oldest estate in Essex.

The abbey in its earliest days was a missionary centre and a double monastery under one abbess. The abbey housed both men and women, though the sexes were segregated. It would take another three hundred years for it to become a female only institution, the only men being priests to conduct mass and laymen to undertake the physical work. The abbey lay deserted for a century after it was sacked by the Danes in 870.

When it was re-founded in the late tenth century by King Edgar it was as a royal foundation, giving the king the power to nominate each new abbess on the death of the old. Exercising his prerogative, Edgar appointed a noblewoman, Wulfhilda, who, in response to his alarming and fervent advances (resulting in a daughter), had fled to Wilton Abbey where she had immediately taken the veil. To make amends for his violence towards her, Edgar also gave the monastery considerable estates. Wulfhilda also bestowed twenty villages of her own upon the abbey.

From this point, date unknown, Barking Abbey became essentially a 'nunnery'. In sharp contrast to the widespread dispossession that took place just after the conquest, Barking's Abbess at the time, Æfgiva, was treated with courtesy. Her abbey's lands were confirmed by William I when he stayed at Barking during the construction of his new stronghold, the Tower of London, on land once owned by the abbey. The abbey's importance was such that it was the venue chosen by William to receive the submission of the northern earls, Edwin of Mercia and his brother Morcar of Northumbria.

Twenty years later, in 1086, the Domesday Book recorded Barking Abbey's land and livestock holdings as seventy-eight hides – approximately 7,800 acres – in thirteen manors in Essex and neighbouring counties. It was to remain one of the wealthiest nunneries in England; its net annual revenues at the time of the Dissolution in 1539 amounted to over £862. In support of this high status, the abbey church, at 100 feet wide and 337 feet high, was described as 'the most splendid of any nunnery in medieval England'.

The abbey's prestige owed much to its close proximity to London. This major source of wealth and power was only ten miles away and contributed queens and princesses to Barking's list of eminent women. Henry I's queen Maud was Abbess for some years before her death in 1118. The wife of King Stephen, Henry II's daughter, and the daughter of King John also held the office.

In the 1170s, Henry II appointed Mary Becket as Abbess in reparation for the murder of her brother, Thomas Becket, the former Archbishop of Canterbury. In 1381, John of Gaunt paid the admission dowry for Elizabeth Chaucy, who became a nun at Barking and was probably a close relative (possibly even the sister) of the poet Chaucer. The aristocracy and members of prominent Essex, Norfolk, and Suffolk families were also represented. In the late thirteenth and early fourteenth centuries, the Abbess Anne de Vere came from the family of the earls of Oxford. In

Barking Abbey Curfew Tower. (*Robert Hallmann*)

the 1340s, Maud de Montague, sister of the Earl of Salisbury, served as Abbess. Her sister, Isabella, succeeded her for six years, and in 1377 there is another Montague as Abbess, this time Maud, Isabella's niece. In the early fifteenth century, the Abbess Margaret Swynford was related by marriage to Thomas, Duke of Exeter, whose name is carved on the keystone of an abbey arch, and who also left the abbey a number of vestments. Katherine de la Pole became Abbess aged twenty-two, holding the office for forty years, from 1433 to 1477. It was the longest tenure in Barking's history.

But new Norman legislation was curtailing women's land holding rights, and out of the sixty-four Benedictine religious houses established after 1066, only three were abbeys. Instead, priories run by a Prioress answerable to an abbott became the norm. But where power from the preceding period devolved on the woman in authority, she kept it. It was from this elevated position that the Abbesses of Barking managed their two-fold income: spiritualities – tithes, gifts, and other ecclesiastical sources of income belonging to the abbey; and temporalities – lands, buildings, and other secular sources of income belonging to abbey estates as far away as Surrey, Buckinghamshire, and Bedfordshire. The five hide manor of Tyburn in Middlesex was the abbey's smallest holding.

Whether a woman entered a monastery for piety or to escape a life of childbearing and ignorance, she would need a sound head for business if she was to fulfil the position of abbess. Between 1175 and 1291, Christiana de Valoniis, Sybil, Mabel de Boseham, Maud, daughter of King John, Christiana de Boseham, Maud de Leveland, and Alice de Merton oversaw the management of agriculture on all abbey lands. They ensured that woodland was harvested for timber and used for pannage, fuel for the abbey and communities was supplied from any peat bogs on the estates, mines were worked for metal deposits, and food was supplied by well-stocked fishponds.

They were also in receipt of various grants and favours. In 1221, licence was granted to Mabel de Boseham to take 'estovers' (any legitimate cutting of timber, for a variety of purposes) and to hunt hares and foxes in her 'wood of Hainault'. Just before Isabel de Basinges was elected in 1291, a grant of free warren in Bedfordshire and Hockley in Essex was given to the abbey, and in 1319 Eleanor de Weston had licence to fell 300 oaks in Hainault for the repair of her manor house, the church, and outbuildings of the abbey, which were in ruins. But with privileges came obligations, and during the years 1385–1463 records show the Abbesses of Barking were responsible for repairing the considerable 'pale' or fence of Havering Park, part of the estate of the Royal Palace.

As the highest authority within Barking Abbey, the rule of St Benedict decreed that:

An abbasse that may be hable & worthy to take vppon hir the Rule & gouernance of a monastery or congregacion / must all wey call to hir rememberaunce & consydre the name of the dignite that she is called by / and labour effectually that hir dedes be accordinge to hir name / and in nothinge contrary to the dignite that she is called / for she occupieth the place of almighty god in the monastery.

She also needed a head for finance as she was responsible for the general funds of the house. These came from the leasing out of Barking mill and lands belonging to the abbey's manors, the collection of rents and taxes in Barking parish, the abbey's wool trade with Holland, plus payments in kind such as grain, produce, wood and hay. Such goods and cash were then used by other officers of the abbey for the daily management of the house. These funds also helped the abbess provide the king with men at arms in time of war, a legal requirement, maintain the abbey as a prison, and handle legal matters which concerned the abbey. In 1291, taxes collected by the abbey amounted to just over £300. One third of this came from Barking itself, the remainder from the Essex parishes of Wigborough, Tollesbury, Hockley, Mucking, Bulphan, and Warley. A little was collected from estates in Middlesex, Surrey and Cambridgeshire. Ingatestone provided the most with £30 14s 11d. By contrast, Abbess Roding only managed £8 17s 4d.

The abbess regularly supervised her stewards in the abbey manor courts; her judgement was sometimes needed to settle disputes. She also oversaw monies paid yearly by the parish priests for their local churches, the advowsons of which were held by the abbey. This applied to the churches of Barking, Dagenham and Horndon on the Hill. In 1315, the church of Mucking was appropriated to the abbey, and a vicarage was ordained. Tollesbury followed in 1355. To supplement the abbess's income when widespread flooding destroyed abbey farmland, Hockley church was licenced in 1382. Next were All Hallows by the Tower in 1385 and Lidlington in 1410. Besides these eight churches, the abbey also owned the advowsons of six rectories, namely, Bulphan, Ingatestone, Abbess Roding, Warley, Wigborough and Slapton. Flood management improved in later years, and through her manor court the abbess was able to impose fines for the failure of her tenants to scour their ditches.

In addition to her responsibilities to the estate, the abbess oversaw the administration of her own household which was separate from the other nuns. It included a cook and kitchen of her own, as well as several personal servants. This privilege sometimes led to abuses. In 1279, Alice de Merton was admonished by Archbishop Peckham for spending too much time in her own apartments and urged her to dine more with her sisters in the convent. Transgressions were rare, but earlier in the twelfth century Archbishop Theobald had to reprimand the Abbess Adelidis (Adeliza) for her 'notorious familiarity and cohabitation' with the abbey's administrator, Hugh of Barking. Lesser complaints against abbesses consisted of favouritism. Dressing too richly and receiving inappropriate gifts were generally dealt with within the abbey walls.

A consequence of the abbess having her own establishment was that the abbey received money for the board and education of young children who, by becoming wards of the abbey, were raised within the abbess' household. Edmund and Jasper Tudor were placed in the custody of the Abbess of Barking from about 1437, when they were aged five and six, to 1440, and Sir John Stanley, in his will of 1528, directed his son and heir to be placed in the abbess's care until he reached the age of twelve. For this Sir John paid £15 annually and a further £20 a year for expenses incurred by his son and his servants.

The second important office in the abbey was that of Prioress; as Barking was an independent establishment, the nun to fill this office was chosen by the abbess herself. The Prioress' role was essentially 'to meyntene religion' and to keep discipline among the nuns and ensure the daily devotions were kept. Barking Abbey was large enough to also have a sub Prioress and a third Prioress. Next in line was the Sacrist, essential to the abbey's liturgical life; it was she who maintained all sacred spaces and objects. In her care were the vestments, provision and care of candles, bells, books, and all of the ornaments used in the abbey's services. At Barking, the Sacrist was aided by the Precentrix, mistress of the choir, and her assistant, the Succentrix, who made sure the ceremonies and chants were carried out correctly by the monastic choristers. Like most offices at Barking, the Sacrist was mistress of her own funds.

After the Sacrist came the office of Cellaress. St Benedict thought this office so important he dictated that the nun for the post should be chosen for her wisdom, good manners, sobriety, humility, quickness, and ability to keep out of trouble. He wrote:

> she shall suffer nothynge / though it be of lyttell value / to goo to waste / nor vnloked to norneclygently [negligently] left or loste.' He further allows that, 'If the conuent be great / she shal haue helpe and comfort of other / by whose socour / she shall do hir duty and office conmytted vnto hir / with a goode wyll / without any grudgynge.

At Barking, the Cellaress was assisted by an under-Cellaress. Between them they were responsible for the abbey's food and supplies. Cellaress was a busy and challenging office to hold; just how challenging can be seen from the pages of *The Charthe longynge to the Office of the Celeresse of the*

Monastery of Barkinge, a book written by a nun early on in the abbey's history in which the Cellaress's duties are meticulously detailed.

> The Celeres schal puruey for mete and drynke for seke and hole, and for mete and drynke, clothe and wages, for seruantes of householde outwarde, and sche shall haue all the vessel and stuffe of housholde under her kepynge and rewle, kepynge it klene, hole and honeste. Ordenying for alle necessaries longynge to al houses of offices concerning the bodily fode of man, in the bakhows, brewhows, kychen, buttry, pantry, celer, freytour, fermery, parlour and suche other, bothe outewarde and inwarde, for straungers and dwellers, attending diligently that the napery and al other thynge in her office be honest, profitable and plesaunte to al, after her power, as sche is commaunded by her souereyne.

As the Cellaress's income derived from the amount that each abbey manor owed her yearly, keeping her accounts in order was vital. This income was used to manage the farm and purchase additional foodstuffs and supplies as necessary. By the later Middle Ages, she had an annual revenue of approximately £98 at her disposal. Part of this income she was allowed to spend on assistants, in addition to her under-Cellaress. At one time, the Cellaress at Barking employed three cooks, a rent collector, and a clerk to help her keep accounts.

Though the Benedictines did not encourage travel, sometimes it was necessary for the Cellaress to leave the abbey to obtain items difficult or impossible to come by any other way. The abbey had its own herd of oxen but at times it was necessary for the Cellaress to supplement their numbers from cattle markets such as those of Smithfield, St Albans, Uxbridge, Dunstable, and Kingston. Other markets visited were London, Cambridge, and Stourbridge in order to purchase large quantities of fish and eels, which was the abbey's staple diet at Lent. If the Cellaress could not travel, she was allowed to appoint a representative. Abbey nuns had a good diet of beef three times a week and pork and mutton less often. In addition to meat and fish, there was bread, ale, oatmeal, butter, eggs, milk, crumb-cakes, chickens, geese, spiced pies and red wine throughout the year and at designated feast times. During Lent, the Cellaress provided the cooks with rice, almonds, figs, raisons, and mustard to add spice to the otherwise bland diet. As these nuns carried out their duties, so too did the fratress, of which Barking Abbey had two. She was in charge of the dining hall and made sure the tables and chairs were clean and in good repair. She also oversaw the purchasing of dishes and tableware.

To hold an office at Barking Abbey, a nun had to be professed for a minimum of seven years, time enough, it was thought, for a nun to have

Eleanor de Bohun was born about 1366 and married Thomas of Woodstock, Duke of Gloucester and son of Edward III. She became a nun at Barking after Thomas was murdered in Calais 1397. She died on 3 October 1399. (*Brass rubbing, Westminster Abbey*)

reached adequate levels of maturity and capability to handle the task. Appointments were made each year on the first Monday of Lent, after the abbess had evaluated the nun's performance over the previous twelve months, praising, rewarding and reappointing those who had performed well, while replacing those who had not. This annual system of review ensured high levels of competence throughout the abbey, making it economically as well as politically strong. Many nuns held their positions for several years, or were promoted to higher offices. Thomasina Jenney, who was Sacrist before 1508, was promoted to Prioress and held that office until the Dissolution in 1539. Margaret Scrope served first as Precentrix in 1527, then as 'lady of the pension' in 1535–6, and finally was sub Prioress at the time of the Dissolution three years later. Length of service was also an indication of competence; in the abbey's last 150 years, every abbess bar two held the office upwards of thirteen years.

Even the lower offices were viewed as positions of responsibility. Barking Abbey was wealthy enough to have a designated librarian who cared for the monastery's books, both religious and secular. This office is thought to have dated from the thirteenth century. At the Dissolution, Barking possessed more than twenty texts and various manuscripts. Other offices listed in Barking's *Ordinale* are: Circuitrices, nuns responsible for daily readings; Searchers, those who scrutinised the abbey and reported disorder to the Prioress; and the Mistress of Novices (referred to as a scolares at Barking), a guide and teacher for the unordained nuns and the Almoness. While not mentioned in Barking's *Ordinale,* the offices of Treasuress, Infirmaress, Chambress and Laundress were probably carried out by committee.

Barking Abbey, like any large manor house, employed outside labourers to perform tasks, even though the rule of St Benedict required the nuns to provide for themselves. Where possible, the abbess would conduct her own business, even riding out on occasion with the benefit of 'sergeantry' (an escort) in order to collect monies or oversee courts. But if duties made that impossible, a steward or bailiff could be nominated to go in her stead. A sixteenth-century abbey account book paid out two sums of three shillings and four pennies to cover the following expenses: 'Payed to Mr. Broke for shoeng of hys horses at dyvers tymes rydyng on my ladyes busyness' and 'Payed for Mr. Pownsettes expenses at London in Ester time for besynes for the howse.'

Hired farm labourers who tended abbey stock were usually paid out of the Cellaress's allowance, while household staff that lived in the abbey were not only paid but often rewarded for their loyalty. The last will of the last Abbess of Barking remembers not only the male servants who worked for her but also their wives who often helped their husbands.

I gyve to Richard Tyllwright my servaunt a trussing of Satten of Brydges with testar and Curtins a fetherbed a boulstar a blew Coverlett with eleven shillings in money. And I gyve to his wiefe one payre of flaxen Shetes a playne table cloth and a single rayle.

I gyve to George Peake somtyme my Servaunt tenne shillings to by hym a cote and to his wiefe a fine playne towel and a single raylle.

I gyve to George Monk somtyme my Servaunt a playne tablecloth and to his wiefe a fine raylle.

A landowner on a large scale, the abbey was run economically and efficiently by the nuns of Barking for almost eight hundred years.

A small entry amongst the letters and papers of Henry VIII is all that marked the end of Barking Abbey: 'Surrender (by Dorothy Barley, Abbess, and the convent) of the monastery and all its possessions in cos. Essex, Midd., Kent, Suss., Surr., Beds, Bucks, Herts, Camb., Suff., Norf., and Linc., the city of London and elsewhere in England.'

Dorothy Barley was the last ever abbess and it was she who surrendered the abbey on 14 November 1539. Small 'alien' houses, mostly French, had been suppressed in the late fourteenth and early fifteenth centuries for avoiding government taxes, but widespread dissolution was something England had never seen.

First to be eliminated were the lesser monasteries with twelve or fewer inmates and annual revenues of £200 or less. Monastic reform was cited as the reason, the details of which were set out in the first few lines of Henry VIII's Act of 1536:

Forasmuch as manifest sin, vicious, carnal, and abominable living is daily used and committed among the little and small Abbeys, priories, and other religious houses of monks, canons, and nuns, where the congregation of such religious persons is under the number of twelve persons, whereby the governors of such religious houses and their convent spoil, destroy, consume, and utterly waste.

As this act went on to describe the larger monasteries as places 'wherin, thanks be to God, religion is right well kept and observed', it appeared Barking Abbey would be saved. But even the abbey's recognition of Henry VIII as head of the English Church in the summer of 1534, and Dorothy Barley's oath of fealty to the king on her election as Abbess in 1527, could not stop the inevitable.

By August 1536, auditors from Henry's 'Court of Augmentations of the Revenues of the King's Crown' – a department created specifically for the purpose of the suppressions – began surveying the remaining monasteries in order to obtain 'induced' surrenders. Many houses yielded to the strong-arm tactics employed, even though some of their methods were essentially outside the law. Other abbesses refused to give up their houses without a fight.

The defiant Abbess of Shaftesbury tried to bribe the king with 100 marks and the king's secretary, Thomas Cromwell, with £100 in order to save her house. The Abbess at Wilton also resisted and only gave up when she had secured a hefty pension for herself of £100, a house with orchards, gardens, and three acres of meadow and pasture, and a weekly load of wood. Records show that there was heroism and obstinacy from both male and female heads of houses, but by far the stiffest resistance came from the women.

Barking was one of the abbeys that made large-scale attempts to save its community by selling property and valuables and granting long-term leases to protect its land. But the government became suspicious and instructed the heads of religious houses that they 'should not, for any such vain babbling of the people, waste, sell, grant or alienate any of their property'. The government took measures and nullified all transactions. The Essex manors owned by the abbey were Barking, Cokermouth in Dagenham, Westbury and Wangey Hall in Barking, Great Warley, Bulphan, Mucking, Hawkesbury in Fobbing, Hockley, Tollesbury, Highall in Tollesbury, Wigborough, Abbes Hall and Caldecotes in Abbess Roding and Leaden Roding, Ingatestone, Wood Barns and Hanley Hall in Ingatestone, and Down Hall.

Sir William Petre was the commissioner who received Barking from its last abbess; for those dependent on the abbey for their livelihood, evidence shows that some received compensation. Of the total £191 paid out to members of all religious houses in Essex, those connected with Barking Abbey received over £50. The abbey buildings fared less well. On 19 June 1541, work commenced 'by his graces commandement in undermynding & casting downe the late Abbey Chyrche of Barking, for the providing of the fayrest coyne stones & other to be ymployed of the Kings man'. This methodical destruction of the abbey continued for eighteen months, finishing in December 1542.

Henry VIII granted the abbey lands and manors to various favourites; in 1539 Sir William Petre bought the Essex property 'Gynge Abbess' or 'Yenge atte Stone', upon which he built Ingatestone Hall in 1540. The abbey site and demesne lands were given to the Earl of Southampton for life.

The valuables stripped from the abbey were substantial. There were huge quantities of lead and bell metal (Barking had eleven bells), in addition to the jewels, silver vessels, silver gilt, parcel gilt, pure silver, copes, gold vestments, and a monstrance (the utensil used for presenting

the consecrated host to the congregation) weighing sixty-five ounces.
There were also 'divers goods, grain and cattle' that were recorded in 1540
as having been sold for just over £182.

As for the nuns, there were thirty in residence with Dorothy Barley
when she surrendered the abbey. She had been abbess since 1527 and had
been at Barking for twenty-one years; she was forty-nine years old. Unlike
nuns from smaller houses, many of whom were reduced to begging, the
nuns at Barking each received an annual pension from the Crown lasting
their lifetime. These pension amounts were calculated by Sir William Petre
who, knowing the abbey's relative wealth, estimated generously. He was
also closely associated with some of the women at Barking, for he had
married Gertrude Tyrell, whose sister Mary Tyrell was one of the last nuns.
Dorothy Barley was also a family friend and godmother to his second
child, a girl named Dorothy, presumably after the abbess. The Abbey had
also favoured Petre in early 1538 by granting him a £10 annuity from
their estates, and this may have influenced the generous pension payment
of £133 6s 8d granted to the abbess.

Thomasina Jenney, the Prioress, received £16 13s 4d, and her sub Prioress
Margaret Scrope was given a pension of £8. Three additional officers were
each given £6 13s 4d. The remaining pensions were split between the more
senior women, receiving £5–6 each, and their juniors receiving 53s 4d. Alice
Hyde, who was probably the youngest of all, received only 33s 4d, a sum
probably attributed to the fact that younger nuns needed lower pensions
because they still had an opportunity to marry after the Dissolution. This
was the case for at least one of them, as Winifred Mordaunt married John
Cheney of Buckinghamshire in the autumn of 1541.

Life for the nuns after the Dissolution was very different from that of
their male counterparts. Monks could continue a life within the Church,
often being paid benefices which supplemented their income. But for the
nuns, their monastic life had ended. Not only had they lost their spiritual
sanctuary, but they could no longer provide the important social services
for their local community. The only serviceable part of the monastery to
survive was the leper hospital founded by the Abbess Adeliza in the twelfth
century at Ilford. It was converted into an almshouse.

Though many women tried to stay together, low pensions eroded by
heavy taxation meant that many women found themselves back with their
secular families in a world they no longer recognised. The daughters of
Sir William Paston and Sir John Shelton both returned to live with their
fathers, as did Mary Tyrell. It is thought Margaret Scrope went to live with
her sister.

Many of the nuns remained ordained until their deaths. In the first round
of dissolutions, Henry VIII's secretary Thomas Cromwell had decreed that

monks and nuns could be freed from their vows only if under the age of twenty-four. By the time his commissioners reached Barking Abbey in 1536, this policy had been extended to include men and women of all ages. The thirty-one nuns present at the Abbey's dissolution three years later proved that few had accepted Cromwell's offer. Many nuns continued to receive their pensions well into Mary I's reign.

Dorothy Barley did not go far after the Dissolution. She retired to the Essex parish of Weald where, as the wording of her will confirms, she continued to be traditionally Catholic. Not until the twentieth century, eight hundred years later, would women again possess the level of power and influence that the nuns of Barking Abbey had enjoyed for themselves and their community.

The Abbesses of Barking Abbey:

Queen Alftrudis
St Wlfhildis (Wulfhilda)
Ælfgiva, c. 1066
Queen Maud, wife of Henry I
Agnes
Queen Maud, wife of Stephen
Adelidis (Adeliza), twelfth century
Mary, appointed in 1173
Maud, daughter of Henry II, appointed c. 1175
Christiana de Valoniis, appointed as acting Abbess on 1202 and 1205
Sybil, elected 1215
Mabel de Boseham, elected 1215, died 1247
Maud, daughter of King John, elected 1247, died 1252
Christiana de Boseham, elected 1252, resigned 1258
Maud de Leveland, elected 1258, resigned 1275
Alice de Merton, 1279
Anne de Vere, died 1318
Eleanor de Weston, elected 1318, died 1329
Yolande de Sutton, elected 1329, died 1341
Maud Montagu, elected 1341, died 1352
Isabel Montagu, elected 1352, died 1358
Katharine de Sutton, elected 1358, died 1377
Maud Montagu, elected 1377, died 1393
Sybil de Felton, or Morle, elected 1393, died 1419
Margaret Swynford, elected 1419, died 1433
Katharine de la Pole, elected 1433, died 1473
Elizabeth Lexham, elected 1473, died 1479

Elizabeth Shuldham, elected 1479, died 1499
Elizabeth Shuldham, elected 1479, died 1499
Elizabeth Grene, elected 1499, died 1527
Dorothy Barley, elected 1527, the last Abbess

MARY BOLEYN, 'LA PETITE BOULLAIN'

Kind, sweet natured, pliable, impulsive and easily manipulated – a woman of easy virtue.

She had lost her lover, the king, to her sister, and was the catalyst of much family advancement, but when she secretly married again for love, after the death of her husband from an arranged childhood marriage, her family turned against her. She was forced to write to the king's secretary, the zealous Thomas Cromwell, for help. But she was the fortunate one; surviving them all, she ultimately inherited the family estates.

These lands were a poignant legacy. They had come to Mary in 1539, she being 'the sole daughter and next heir' of her father, Sir Thomas, Earl of Ormond and Wiltshire. Had her brother lived, the family fortunes would undoubtedly have passed to him. But George had been beheaded on Tower Hill on the morning of Wednesday, 17 May 1536. Her sister Anne, also by the king's decree, had met her death two days later, charged, like George, with 'illicit intercourse', treason and incest. Considering her own fall from grace, it was a prudent Mary Carey who retired to Rochford Hall, deep in the Essex countryside. Now the only surviving child of the ambitious Thomas and his wife Katherine Howard, she was mistress of considerable landholdings in Essex and Norfolk.

Mary's individual character is not well known. Contemporary accounts considered her prettier than her sister, she being as fair as Anne was dark, and, until the tumultuous life of her sister overshadowed her own, Mary had been the most famous member of the 'Bullen' family.

Mary's journey into notoriety began at a tender age. Though she did not attend the court of Margaret of Savoy, Archduchess of Austria when Thomas Bullen was appointed Ambassador in 1512, Mary did cross the channel with Henry VIII's sister, the eighteen-year-old Mary Tudor, who, in marrying the aged Louis XII, was to become queen of France. Mary was too young to be given such a position as Maid of Honour, but her age saved 'Ma petite Boullain' as the French queen affectionately called her, at a time when the king ordered the queen's ladies from Court.

Three months later, Mary Tudor was a widow and had returned to England. Mary Bullen now found herself in the polarised and duplicitous

Mary Boleyn, later Mary Carey, and lastly Mary Stafford.

court of Francis I. Here she existed between a realm of pious maidens – raised solely to do needlework and attend chapel – and a bawdy and licentious array of mistresses to the young king. By fifteen years of age she too had caught the French king's eye, not to mention those of several of his courtiers. 'Spirited, sweet, fresh and winning' according to one account, she was christened by the king as his 'English mare' in reference to the number of times he had 'ridden' her. In later years he was to say she was 'una grandissima ribalda, et infamme supra tutte' – 'a great whore and infamous above all others'. It is possible that Francis I meant to discredit the King of England more than his former mistress with these ungallant remarks. In the political games of one-upmanship that were constantly taking place between two of the sixteenth century's greatest Renaissance princes, no opportunity was overlooked to gain an advantage.

That Henry VIII was enchanted by Mary's light-hearted and uncalculating personality is not in dispute. Mary's wedding to William Carey on 4 February 1520, a dynastic marriage arranged years before, was attended by Henry VIII, who made the couple a gift of six shillings and eight pence. Mary was to meet the king again later that year when her family attended the Anglo-French spectacle her father had helped arrange as the newly appointed French ambassador. Here, on the 'Field of the cloth of Gold,' the festivities lasted from 7 to 23 June and both Bullen girls, Anne as 'une fille d'honor' to the French queen, were introduced to their Sovereign. Whether by chance or design, it was Mary who made the greatest impression at that time.

A year later, when Anne was recalled to England from France, Mary had already embarked upon a six-year association with the king. As if in recognition of his affair with Mary, the king bestowed grants upon her husband, a gentleman of the privy chamber, settling upon him two keeperships, a stewardship, an annuity, and manors in two counties. Carey also received royal grants each year from 1522 to 1525. Mary's father, too, rose rapidly in the realm, becoming Treasurer of the Household, Ambassador to Spain, and Clerk of the King's Jewels. In 1523, the royal ship *Mary Bullen* was launched, bought by Henry from Thomas, his newly created Knight of the Garter. Elevated to the peerage, Thomas Bullen also became Viscount Rochford in 1525. In the same year he was made Keeper of the King's Park at Thundersley.

The birth of a first child, a son, in 1524 did not seriously affect the king's relationship with Mary. The child's physical resemblance to the king led to assumptions by many that it was the king's son. In 1535 for example, the vicar of Iselworth, John Hale, called 'young master Carey' the king's son 'by our suffren Lady the Qwyen's sister'. Henry chose not to acknowledge the boy as his own, although he did provide generously for the child when Mary returned to her husband, and after her husband's death of sweating sickness in 1528, an influenza-type epidemic brought on by an especially hot summer. By this time, Henry's passions were becoming firmly fixed upon Anne. At Court, the birth of Mary's second child, Catherine, went almost unnoticed.

Newly widowed, no longer useful to her father, and an embarrassment to Anne, who feared a descent back into obscurity like her sister, Mary fell from favour. By September 1527, Henry had already taken his first steps to secure a divorce from Catherine of Aragon. In order to make Anne his queen, he also had to disassociate himself from Mary, whom he had taken in 'forbidden wedlock'. Without her son, custody of whom went to Anne, and her deceased husband's sources of income, which the king had given away, Mary faced poverty in the midst of an opulent court.

Her secret marriage in 1534 to William Stafford, the younger son of a Midland family whose fortunes had been greatly depleted, did nothing to ease Mary's situation. Conscious of their rising social status and outraged at such a social disgrace, the newly named 'Boleyn' family banished Mary and William from Court. Retiring to the Essex countryside, Mary had to watch her father Thomas and brother George receive privileges and titles, while she was reduced to imploring Thomas Cromwell, Henry VIII's chief minister, for assistance. Signing herself Mary Stafford she wrote,

> But one thing, good master Secretary, consider that he was young and love overcame reason. And for my part I saw so much honesty in him that I loved him as well as he did me; and was in bondage and glad I was to be at liberty; so that for my part I saw that all the world did set so little by me, and he so much, that I thought I could take no better way but to take him and forsake all other ways and to live a poor and honest life with him; and so I do put no doubt but we should if we might once be so happy to recover the King's gracious favour and the Queen's. For well I might have of had a better man of birth and higher, but I swear to you, I could never a had one that loved me so well, nor a more honest man.

She also asks Cromwell to speak to the queen who is 'so rigorous' against them:

> We have been now a quarter of a year married, I thank God, and too late now to call that again ... I had rather beg my bread with him than to be the greatest Queen christened ... pray my Lord my father and my Lady to be good to us ... and my Lord of Norfolk and my brother ... I dare not write to them, they are so cruel against us.

Mary's insignificant marriage and banishment from Court ultimately protected her from the tragedy that was to befall her siblings and bring about her father's ruin. But the king, it seemed, had not completely forgotten 'la petite Boullain'. In an unusual business transaction that took place after the disgraced Thomas Boleyn had died at his Norfolk home in 1539, Hever Castle, instead of reverting automatically to the crown, was 'sold' to the king by Mary's uncle, Sir James Bullen. As recorded in the patent rolls, a sum of money was paid to Mary Stafford.

The reason for the king's gift is unrecorded, but it marked a period of subsequent good fortune for Mary during the years 1539–42. As well as her father's lands, Mary also found herself mistress of estates held jointly with her brother George's widow, Jane Rochford, and the lands of her grandmother, the Countess of Ormonde. An 'inquisition postmortem',

taken at around the time of Mary's death, showed that she owned lands all
over Essex, from the 'Roothings' in the north, to the marshes and islands
of Foulness way down in the south of the county. As Lady Rochford, Mary
also held the advowson of the churches of 'Pakelsham', 'Hakewell', and
'Lighe' (Pagglesham, Hawkwell, and Leigh), and the Honour of Rayleigh.

The inquisition details Mary's holdings in Essex as: 1,000 messuages,
1,000 cottages, ten watermills, ten windmills, 20,000 acres of land, 20,000
acres of meadow, 15,000 acres of pasture, 3,000 acres of wood, 10,000
acres of furze and heath, 20,000 acres of marsh, and £100 in rent. She was
also the owner of 100 dovehouses, one of which she expressly ordered to
be built at her home, Rochford Hall, in 1540. Circular, with a thatched
roof, it stood, according to local historian Philip Benton, 'in a meadow to
the south of the hall'. In 1888 it was eventually struck by lightning and
had to be pulled down.

Rochford Hall, the estate Mary Boleyn inherited after her family's death. Not far
from this spot stood the dovecot Mary commissioned, which stood until the late
1890s. (*Robert Hallmann*)

Throughout Mary's life, Rochford Hall, with its gabled roofs and twisted chimneys, had been both her exile and refuge. It was here that she died on 19 July 1543, leaving Henry, her son by her marriage to William Carey, as beneficiary. Still a minor at seventeen years old, his affairs were managed by his stepfather, William Stafford, who lived for another twelve to thirteen years at the hall, even marrying again.

Mary Boleyn's real legacy was in her childrens' services to Queen Elizabeth I, her sister Anne's daughter. Catherine Carey became gentlewoman of the Privy Chamber at Elizabeth's accession; she married Sir Francis Knollys, and became the grandmother of Lord Essex, the queen's favourite in her later years. Henry Carey, 1st Lord of Hunsdon, served as the queen's trusted advisor and put down the Catholic Dacre rebellion against Elizabeth in February 1570. On that occasion, the queen wrote Henry Carey a touching letter of which his mother Mary Boleyn would have been proud:

I doubt much, my Harry, whether that the victory were given me, more joyed me, or that you were by God appointed the instrument of my glory; and I assure you that for my country's good, the first might suffice, but for my heart's contention the second pleased me ... you have done much for honour ... Your loving kinswoman, Elizabeth R.

QUEENS WHO HELD ESSEX IN THEIR DOWRIES

Many women, even foreign queens, have received the county of Essex, or parts of it, as a gift. Margaret, the sister of Philip IV of France and second wife of King Edward I, was given Hadleigh Castle, built in 1230, and its estates in 1299 as part of her dower. It was also part of the marriage contract between the so called 'She-Wolf of France', Queen Isabella, and her husband Edward II.

It soon became the custom for Hadleigh Castle to be granted to a tenant for a lifetime, then revert back to the crown at his or her death. By tradition, the tenant was usually the king's consort. In 1314, Queen Margaret complained that 'divers persons had entered her parks, free chases and free warrens of Hadley and hunted therein without her license. Also in like manner entered her closes, there broke her houses, walls and fences, fished in her stew and free fisheries, carried away her trees and fish and took deer from her park and hares, rabbits, pheasants and partridges.'

Most notably, the stronghold belonged to three of King Henry VIII's wives – Catherine of Aragon, Anne of Cleves and Catherine Parr. Anne Of Cleves, the queen who was so quickly married and even more quickly divorced, was happy to renounce her marriage to the King of England

Hadleigh Castle was among many Essex estates given by English monarchs to royal women as part of their dowries. Three of Henry VIII's wives held Hadleigh Castle, namely Catherine of Aragon, Anne of Cleves, and Catherine Parr. Almost three centuries before, in 1299, Margaret, the sister of Philip IV of France, laid claim to the stronghold. It also formed part of the marriage contract between the so-called 'She-Wolf of France', Queen Isabella, and her husband Edward II. (*Robert Hallmann*)

and accept, as part of her allowance, the Fishery of Hadleigh Ray and the 'dragging of muscles at Tilbury Hope'. A year later, the manors of Hockley and Pagglesham were added, as well as some marshes at Canewdon.

In 1267, the palace, village, forest, woodland, pastures, and marshes of Havering near Romford became the property of the queens of England, though it was always known as the 'King's House and Park at Havering'. Queen Eleanor first held it as part of her dower, and the suffix 'atte-bower' denoted this was where the queen often resided. Eleanor is warmly remembered by history as the queen who inspired the Eleanor crosses – twelve lavishly decorated stone monuments, erected by her husband Edward I to mark the nightly resting places of her body on its way to be buried in London. She was not, however, so loved in her own time. The English saw her as a greedy foreigner with a keen eye for land acquisition; between 1274 and 1290 she acquired estates worth over £2,500 yearly. In the words of a contemporary poem, 'The king desires to get our gold, the queen, our manors fair to hold'.

The development of the Palace of Havering was somewhat haphazard, with each monarch adding to an increasing jumble of buildings. It is reputed to have had one of the first baths installed by Henry II for the use of his royal lady. It was also the favourite palace of Queen Joan of Navarre, the wife of Henry IV, and where she died in 1238.

2

ROYAL WOMEN IN ESSEX

'BLOODY' MARY TUDOR (1516–1558)

Mary in her youth did not lack charm. She was by nature modest, affectionate, and kindly.

It is hard to believe a woman who put almost 300 Protestants to death in her brief reign was ever modest, affectionate, and kindly. But contemporary accounts of Mary in her youth bear this out, citing the harsh treatment she received during Anne Boleyn's ascendancy as responsible for hardening her heart. Indeed, Mary lived under the constant threat of death as Anne was intent in bringing both Catherine of Aragon and her daughter Mary to the gallows. Such strain was only alleviated once Anne had been executed and Jane Seymour had taken her place. In Jane, Mary at last found a woman who would befriend her.

Mary spent time at New Hall near Chelmsford on two occasions. The first was during the troubled times of her father's divorce from her mother, Catherine of Aragon. The second was when the magnificent building was given to her 'for life' by her brother Edward.

Her second visit was a time of obscurity for Mary. Her father, Henry VIII, had died in January 1547, and her Catholicism was a thorn in the side of the new regime which surrounded her brother Edward, the new king. Strangely, this was made worse by the fact that she had found favour with the last of her father's wives, Catherine Parr, who, wishing to make amends to Mary, persuaded the king to reinstate his first natural daughter in his will, naming her as successor to the throne after little Edward.

Mary had now become a rallying point, a figurehead for the Catholic faction, an object of derision for the Protestants. On several occasions, when loyal followers felt her life to be in danger, they would move her secretly to Woodham Walter and place her in the care of the Fitzwalters,

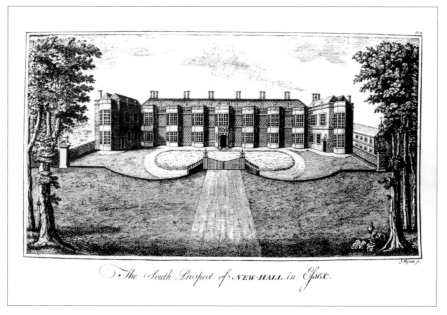

The South Prospect of NEW-HALL in Essex.

New Hall, where Mary spent many years in seclusion while issues of the succession played out about her. Ironically for Mary, New Hall had been bought by her father, Henry VIII, from Thomas Boleyn, the father of the woman who had so blighted her life. (*Essex Record Office*)

a prominent Essex family. Should a threat become too real, a boat was constantly kept ready at Maldon to carry her to the continent.

After the early death of her brother and the nine-day reign of Lady Jane Grey, Mary finally became Queen of England in 1553; four short years later, she died childless. Mary's first act was to repeal the Protestant legislation of her brother, Edward VI, hurling England into a phase of severe religious persecution. Her major goal was the re-establishment of Catholicism in England, a goal to which she was totally committed. Persecution came more from a desire for purity in faith rather than vengeance, yet the fact remains that nearly 300 people (including Thomas Cranmer, the former Archbishop of Canterbury, and many of the most prominent members of society) were burned at the stake for heresy, earning Mary the nickname 'Bloody Mary'.

Ironically for Mary, New Hall, where she spent so much time in seclusion, had been bought by her father from Thomas Boleyn, the father of the woman who had so blighted her life.

With Essex not usually the life-long home of many of England's monarchs, its varied coastline and proximity to the continent made it the transient abode of many of the royal line. After her victory over the Scots,

Queen Phillipa, wife of Edward III, was entertained at New Hall by the Abbott of Waltham. Similarly, Margaret of Anjou, Henry VI's queen, also stayed at the hall.

ELIZABETH I, A LADY OF 'PROGRESS' (1533–1603)

When it pleaseth her in the summer season to recreate herself abroad, and view the state of the country, every nobleman's house is her palace.
(William Harrison, *Description of England*)

What constitutes an Essex Girl? For our purposes it's not necessarily just the accident of birth. Although not born in Essex, Queen Elizabeth I did spend much of her childhood in Havering-atte-Bower, an Essex palace which later became the starting off or finishing point for many of her travels. During her captivity as a young princess, she had also lived in many Essex country houses; her nomadic lifestyle, with spells in the Tower, taught her just how fickle public opinion could be. It was a lesson well learned. Once queen, Elizabeth decided that England's prosperity and her power would be based upon the love and devotion of her people; she was determined to make royal popularity the cornerstone of her reign. The great Elizabethan 'progress' was the mechanism behind this lifelong public relations exercise. Every spring and summer of her forty-four-year reign she moved among her people and made sure she was seen by them, even if the contrast between their lifestyles and hers was quite incomparable. In doing so, she successfully made her subjects her greatest asset. They in turn could see for themselves what a great queen she was.

And what was she like, the Virgin Queen? We have the French Ambassador's report to the French king in 1595, when her half-sister Queen Mary still occupied the throne.

> She [Elizabeth] is tall with a good skin ... she has fine eyes and above all, beautiful hands ... Her intellect and understanding are wonderful ... Proud and haughty, as although she knows she was born of such a mother, she nevertheless does not consider herself of inferior in degree to the Queen, whom she equals in self-esteem; nor does she believe herself less legitimate than her Majesty, alleging in her own favour that her mother would never cohabit with the King unless by way of marriage, with the authority of the Church ... She prides herself on her father and glories in him; everybody saying that she also resembles him more than the Queen does and he therefore always liked her and had her brought up in the same way as the Queen.

Elizabeth I by Nicholas Hilliard, 1585. When Elizabeth I went on her 'Progresses', she would take the whole of her court with her, usually consisting of up to 300 wagons and a similar number of staff. In some instances, courtiers were left bankrupt after having to accommodate the Queen. (*Photograph by kind permission of Hatfield House*)

An Englishman's home may have been his castle, but not exclusively. All manors in the land ultimately belonged to the Sovereign, an ancient feudal right which meant she could occupy the house of any subject anywhere at any time. For many, this was a chance to impress, an honour to be savoured, and a boost for local pride, even if the expenses incurred might cripple the host. There was no redress for being brought near to ruin by the queen's 'progress', for, however difficult or tedious such a journey, there was no compromise on comfort; much of her furniture and even the royal bed had to be carted along.

As Elizabeth seldom set foot more than twenty miles outside of London, these summer forays into the English countryside were also a chance to escape the stifling heat, smells and outbreaks of plague in the city – London theatres closed during these months for just that reason. She would lodge with nobles and gentry in her bid to be seen by many and to win people's hearts. She also made a considerable saving on royal household expenses.

Elizabeth made in excess of four hundred visits to individual and civic hosts. Between 1558 and 1603, towns were obliged and honoured to welcome her; entertaining the queen could not be avoided.

While Essex has no unique claim on Elizabeth, it was a well-favoured destination. In Essex, the queen visited the ancient boroughs of Maldon, Colchester, Harwich and Saffron Walden. She was entertained by Sir William Petre of Ingatestone Hall, Sir Thomas Mildmay of Moulsham, Chelmsford (Sir Thomas is recorded as having complained of the expense), and Lord Darcy of St Osyth. Other great houses were visited at Epping, Great Hallingbury, Ongar, Kelvedon, Gosfield and Abbess Roothing. At Horham Hall, Thaxted, Elizabeth stayed for as long as nine days.

Elizabeth did not travel light. She insisted that the decor and ambiance of the royal palaces at Greenwich, Whitehall, Richmond and Hampton Court were recreated in the halls and dining rooms of her hosts; all her furniture, wall hangings, books, pictures, jewels, bedlinen, including the royal bed, had to be moved in with her. A baggage train of at least three to four hundred carts was needed, the whole entourage spanning on average a distance of ten miles from the first wagon to the last – surely an excursion to be noticed. If lucky, her hosts would be told of her forthcoming visit months in advance and were able to vacate their homes, leaving only an empty shell for the queen and her court to occupy. If notice was less generous, or the venue a brief stay with minor gentry 'en route', then it was a wise host who made himself scarce and let the 'officers of the chamber' take over the premises lock, stock and barrel.

Elizabeth had the final say on her 'progress', but the planning was left to the Privy Council and the Lord Chamberlain. His responsibility was to the queen and the accommodation of her immediate attendants, which left the rest of the royal entourage to fend for themselves. Lodging houses in the vicinity of the royal progress were rapidly taken (a chance for the owners to inflate prices and line their own pockets) and when those had been snapped up, tents were put up in the fields and meadows all around – like a miniature Tudor Woodstock.

While the logistics of travel were one aspect to be organised by the queen's entourage, the matter of sustenance fell to the host. Kitchens and cellars needed to be stocked in the manner to which the royal visitor was accustomed. Ingatestone, the brick-built residence of Sir William Petre, was one of the stops in the summer of 1561, during a 'progress' that had begun on 14 July at Wanstead House, the Earl of Leicester's residence.

Elizabeth arrived at Ingatestone Hall on Friday 19 July and stayed for five days. Sir William was a Devon man with a double degree in canon and civil law at Oxford, who had risen to become a deputy of Thomas Cromwell under the queen's father. He later served Edward VI and Mary Tudor as principal secretary. He has been described as a 'new man': someone who bent, rather than broke, however the wind blew. In fact, the Dictionary of National Biography describes him as being 'sprung from the willow rather than the oak'. He was now one of Elizabeth's principal secretaries, a senior royal servant, and a man of substance, owning 20,000 acres in Essex alone. Obviously his hospitality needed to match his position. His account book meticulously listed the expenses incurred, including Lady Petre's purchase of '13 ells of green taffeta sarcenet' for lining curtains, and a quarter pound of 'fusses', perhaps a Tudor pot pourri for perfuming the royal chambers. What could not be provided from the rabbit-warrens, dovecots, fishponds, and store rooms of the tenants on his estate had to be bought and transported from London.

A Declarac[i]on of all suche p[ro]vision of victualls and other nessesaries as was bought and p[ro]vided against the quenes Ma[jes]tes cominge to my M[aste]rs howse at yngatstone beinge the xixth day of Julye the thirde yere of her Ma[jes]tes Reigne and there tar[y]inge untill the xxijth of the same both daies included.

Some of the provisions on that list may interest today's housewives, chefs, and naturalists. Besides all the 'white wheate', 'brede', 'beare & ale', there were 'sea fishe' such as soles, flounders, 'gurnardes', congers and 'sturgion'. Perhaps more surprising are six 'signettes' (young swans), plus four 'signettes' and six 'bitters' from Cambridge, six dozen 'pewettes', a dozen gulls, two dozen 'brewes' (a kind of snipe, a medium sized wading bird), two dozen 'egrettes', twelve dozen 'quailes' from London, equally twelve herons and twelve 'shoulvlers' (spoonbill ducks), plus another eighteen herons and twelve 'shoulvlers' from Kent. Added to that were sums for presents, and the dozen capons and two dozen 'chekins' for Sir William's own table.

How the Petres felt about the hole in their pocket left by their sovereign's visit is not known, but by 5 August Elizabeth had left Ingatestone, in her cumbersome and springless coach, and arrived at Ipswich, the furthermost point of that 'progress'. They had followed a circular route on the great eastern road and thence through northern Essex by way of Hedingham, Leeze Priory (her visit with Lord Riche costing him £389), Great Hallingbury and on into Hertford.

It was not always a pleasure for her hosts, nor was it unheard of for nobles to absent themselves from Court in order to avoid being visited. It was not unusual to suffer financial ruin following such an event. You could not slight the queen by being frugal with your provisions, but making her too welcome might backfire as well, as Sir John Cutte of Horham Hall near Thaxted discovered. So impressed was the queen with Sir John's hospitality on her two visits, one which had lasted nine days in 1571, the other for six days in 1578, that she subsequently sent the Spanish Ambassador with his numerous attendants to stay at Horham Hall during an outbreak of plague in London. Alas, Sir John could not afford the extra expense and eventually had to sell off Horham, moving near to Cambridge.

Providence occasionally smiled upon a prospective host, a case in point being Lord Darcy of St Osyth, but not before preparations had been made. Arriving on 30 July 1561, the queen encountered a 'great thunder and lightning as any man had ever heard till past 10, then great rain till midnight ... the people thought the world was at an end, and the day of doom come.' The storm caused such panic and alarm that the queen decided she should move on straight away!

Naturally, the business of state could not be neglected during the queen's absence, so the Council accompanied her as part of the court routine, conducting its business wherever she stayed. Special arrangements might have to be implemented to receive and dispatch their reports and instructions. During the queen's stay at Audley End in July 1578, the Council convened at nine meetings. Lord Burleigh was present, the Scottish Ambassador had talks, and foreign courtiers were received.

While her Lord Chamberlain and Vice-Chamberlain were responsible for detailed preparation and management, the 'harbingers' travelled ahead to look for suitable lodgings. The plague was the great curse of the time and mayors of towns and lord-lieutenants of counties had to confirm its absence when the queen's 'gestes' or itineraries were published and their area was favoured. Stocks of fuel, food and, of course, fodder for the horses had to be provided by towns and villages along the way, a necessity for which a Yeoman Purveyor and a deputy were assigned a Royal Commission 'to take up and provide for us'.

Elaborate preparations might have to be made when a town received notice of the queen's intended visit. If notice was generous enough, there might be time to spruce up the town and have every house newly painted, including the market cross. Stocks, pillory and cage, normally used to punish malefactors, might have to be removed.

The roads were often rutted and potholed; as they tended to be the responsibility of the parish through which they ran, pressure for their improvement might have to be brought to bear. Even so, streets were strewn with rushes or gravel. Muck hills and middens would be removed so as not to offend her majesty, and herbs might disguise troublesome odours. Cows were forbidden into town during the time of a visit.

Flags flew and 'suche lyke, every howse adorned with green boughs'. Bells rang out at the queen's passing. According to the Chelmsford churchwarden's accounts, 6s 8d was paid to the ringers when the queen came through the town.

Entry into a town would be a great ceremonial occasion. With townsfolk cheering, the queen was received by bailiffs and burgesses and she politely listened to speeches by town recorders. Gifts expressing loyalty and affection would be offered to the queen, and, though she professed she came for 'the hearts and allegiance of her subjects', she nevertheless accepted them gracefully. At Audley End in July 1578, having been entertained by officials and students from nearby Cambridge University, Elizabeth was presented with a particular favourite, a pair of scented gloves. Opening the gift, 'hir Majestie behoulding the beautie of the said gloves, as in great admiration, and in token of hir thankfull acceptation of the same, held up one of her hands; and then, smelling into them, putt them half waie upon hir hands.'

During the 'summer progress' of 1561, Elizabeth visited Dovercourt and Harwich. Silas Taylor, storekeeper at the Naval Yard, writing almost a century later, reported on the queen's visit:

August 12, 1561, Queen Elizabeth came hither and accepted of an Entertainment from the Borough, lodging, as it is said, for several days at a House about the middle of the High-Street, and being attended by the Magistrates at her Departure as far as the Windmill out of Town, she graciously demanded of them, what they had to request of her, from whom she received this Answer, Nothing, but to wish her Majesty a good journey: Upon which she turned her Horse about, and looking upon the Town said, *A pretty Town and wants nothing*, and so bad them farewell.

Later, Queen Elizabeth's 'sea-hawks', Frobisher, Hawkins, and Drake, would set sail on various expeditions from this north Essex harbour, Hawkins himself commanding a small flotilla of the 'the queenes shippes' out of Harwich in 1588 to engage the Spanish Armada.

Elizabeth's best known visit to Essex was to Tilbury at the anticipation of that very Armada. In May 1588, the Spanish had been sighted off Cornwall and were subsequently defeated and scattered off Gravelines. On 9 August, Elizabeth I famously addressed her troops at Tilbury. Every schoolboy knows her proud and rousing words:

> I am come amongst you all, to lay down my life for my God and for my kingdom and for my people, my honour, and my blood, even in the dust. I know I have the body of a weak and feeble woman, but I have the heart and stomach of a king, and of a king of England too.

Dr Leonel Sharp had good reason to remember the day the Queen rode 'as armed Pallas, attended by noble footmen, Leicester, Essex, and Norris, then Lord Marshall, and divers other great lords'. Sometime after 1623, Dr Sharp recalled the queen's words in a letter to the Duke of Buckingham, presumably accurately, because he'd had to repeat her oration to the troops the following day – after her departure – to ensure they were heard by everyone.

Elizabeth's rousing speech had certainly swelled the hearts of her troops, but equally left the churchwardens of West Tilbury with a bill for damage done by so large a body of men called to arms. Accused by the archdeacon of neglecting their church wall and furniture, the churchwardens replied 'that church stooles and walls is muche broken downe by means of the campe that did lie there', adding that, 'there were non at Tilbury campe but Rogues and Rascals'. For such remarks aimed at the queen's patriots, the churchwardens were ordered to repair the damage at their own expense!

A charming conversation with the wife of Elizabeth's godson, Sir John Harrington, has been recorded, reflecting the depth of the queen's belief in the love of her subjects. It is also a poignant reminder that Elizabeth's royal life conflicted on so many levels with that of her own personal happiness. When asking the young woman how she kept the love of her husband, the woman replied, by dealing with him gently, not denigrating him or crossing him so he was assured of her love for him. The queen likened herself to a wife in her marriage with the people when she replied, 'go to, go to, mistress. You are wisely bent, I find; after such sort do I keep the good-will of my husbands, my good people; for if they did not rest assured of some special love towards them, they would not readily yield me such good obedience.'

MARIE DE MEDICI (1573–1642)

She surrounds herself with busy-bodies.

(Charles I)

Amid a degree of pomp and circumstance, Catherine De Medici, widow of Henry IV of France, mother of Louis XIII, and mother-in-law of Charles I, arrived uninvited in England in 1638 for an impromptu and lengthy stay. Charles, in the middle of a political and personal crisis, had little time, or desire, to accommodate his wife's mother. He was not alone. Known to be a most meddlesome woman, even her son King Louis XIII had driven her out of France and into exile in Brussels. Such was Charles I's dislike for the French dowager that, upon hearing she wanted to come and live in England, he had offered the complete resources of the navy to take her elsewhere, suggesting Italy or Spain.

Catherine was to visit England from Holland. She had been a year in Brussels, but having outstayed her welcome there she needed to move on. Rather than slam the doors of England in his mother-in-law's face, Charles acted the dutiful son-in-law and rode out to greet his unwelcome guest on her journey from Harwich to London. They met at Sir Henry Mildmay's house in Moulsham Hall, Chelmsford, on 8 November 1638. The encounter was 'correct', even superficially cordial, but was later in sharp contrast to his wife's (Henrietta Maria's) obvious joy at seeing the mother she had missed for thirteen years.

From Chelmsford, Charles escorted his formidable mother-in-law towards London. They rode in two long trains of coaches and horsemen (it is rumoured that Marie's household consisted of almost 600 Frenchmen), preceded by twelve trumpeters.

That night, the queen slept at Gidea Hall, Romford, while Charles stayed at Havering. As the royal palace at Havering was now in an increasing state of decay, Charles had thought it prudent to house Marie de Medici at the more prestigious accommodation, meeting up with her entourage the next morning to continue the journey into London.

Charles never really got on with his mother-in-law; he was known to have thought her 'a constant expense', and a barrier between him and his wife!

Charles I was none-too-enamoured with his mother–in-law, Marie de Medici. He
thought her 'meddlesome', and that she kept the company of 'busy-bodies'.

CATHERINE OF BRAGANZA (1638–1705)

Her face is not so exactly as to be called a beauty, though her eyes are excellent good, and nothing in her face that in the least degree can disgust one. On the contrary, she hath as much agreeableness in her looks as I ever saw, and if I have any skill in physiognomy, which I think I have, she must be as good a woman as ever was born. You will wonder to see how well we are acquainted already; in a word, I think myself very happy, for I am confident our two humours will agree very well together.

(Charles II)

Audley End became a royal residence in 1668 when it was purchased by Charles II as a base for attending Newmarket races. It was also used by James II and William and Mary. When it was built in 1614 it was the largest house in England, and James I joked that it was too big for a King but not for a Lord Treasurer!

Queen Catherine of Braganza held court at Audley End in the autumn of 1668. Chronically shy at times, she would escape to this house in the country as a change from her life in London, her childlessness, and the king's many mistresses. Once, disguised as country lass in a red petticoat and waistcoat, the queen went 'a frolicking' to Walden fair, (Saffron Walden) with the Duchess of Richmond and the Duchess of Buckingham. Unfortunately, the aristocratic ladies had overdone it in their costumes and according to a correspondence between two gentlemen some years later they 'looked more like antiques than country folk'. Their apparel drew the attention of the crowd and so the queen momentarily slipped into a booth to buy a pair of yellow stockings 'for her sweetheart', while a young man in their party slipped into another booth to purchase a pair of gloves 'stitched with blew' for *his* sweetheart. Before long the royal party were rediscovered by their foreign 'gibberish'. One man, recognising Her Majesty and empowered by his excitement, said he had seen her 'at dinner and was proud of it'. Unfortunately, this caused the whole fair to come and stare at Catherine; not wanting to be the centre of such attention, she and the royal revellers then took to their horses. Unused to having such a royal in their midst the crowd followed suit 'with their wives, children, sweethearts and neighbours behind them to get as mush gape as they could till the weight of the following horses brought the queen and her ladies to the Court gate.'

There was no malice in the crowd's intent. They had only thought to see a queen go 'a-fairing', a merry sight. The letter concluded on a more sober note. 'Thus by ill contrivance was a merry frolick turned into a pennance.'

Catherine of Braganza (1638–1705), queen consort of Charles II of England, daughter of John IV of Portugal. She was married to Charles in 1662.

CHARLOTTE OF
MECKLENBURG-STRELITZ (1744–1818)

The English people did not like me much, because I was not pretty.

Princess Charlotte landed in Harwich in 1761 on her way to marry George III, having been chosen as his bride on his accession in 1760. A small flotilla of yachts and men-of-war under the Admiral of the Fleet Lord Anson was sent to Cuxhaven on the German coast to collect the Princess. The principal yacht, *Royal Caroline*, had been renamed *Royal Charlotte* and sumptuously fitted out for the Princess in her honour. It should have been a straightforward escort exercise, but such were the westerly gales at the time that the returning vessels were blown over to the Norwegian coast three times, taking the party ten days to reach Harwich.

Serres, England's leading marine painter, visited Harwich in September 1761 to record the arrival of the Princess; his picture shows this much delayed event in Harwich harbour, with sunlight breaking through the clouds onto the *Royal Charlotte* as she passes Landguard Fort.

The Hon. Horace Walpole, in a letter to the Earl of Stratford, described Charlotte's eventual arrival, declaring there had never been such a bustle about the town of Harwich as there had been lately.

> The Queen was seen off the coast of Sussex on Saturday last, and is not arrived yet – nay, last night at ten o'clock it was neither certain when she landed, nor when she would be in town ... Five, six, seven, eight o'clock came, and no Queen ... She lay at Witham at Lord Abercorn's, who was most tranquilly in town; and it is not certain even whether she will be composed enough to be in town to-night. She has been sick but half an hour; sung and played on the harpsichord all the voyage, and been cheerful the whole time. The coronation will now certainly not be put off.

In a last correspondence, Walpole confirmed to his friend,

> Madame Charlotte is this instant arrived. The noise of the coaches, chaises, horsemen, mob, that have been to see her pass through the parks, is so prodigious that I cannot distinguish the guns. I am going to be dressed, and before seven shall launch into the crowd. Pray for me!

Seventeen years later, on 19 October 1778, Charlotte passed through Brentwood with her husband George III to visit Robert, ninth Lord Petre, at his new mansion of Thorndon Park in order to inspect the troops.

Princess Charlotte of Mecklenburg-Strelitz landed in Harwich in 1761 on her way
to marry George III. It had taken ten days to complete the normally easy crossing
from her home in Germany as gale-force winds blew them towards the Norwegian
coast at least three times.

She, along with her husband, was given a tumultuous welcome by the townspeople and the road was lined with soldiers. At the hall there was a grand dinner party and firework display. It is not clear whether Charlotte accompanied him, but the next day the king went on to Warley, three miles south of Brentwood, where six years earlier a temporary military camp had been set up on Warley Common. Here the king reviewed his troops and witnessed a mock battle. When he left Thorndon, he gave Lord Petre 100 guineas for the servants and left money for the poor at Brentwood.

CAROLINE AMELIA ELIZABETH OF BRUNSWICK (1768–1821)

Pretty face – not expressive of softness – figure not graceful – tolerable teeth but going – fair hair and light eyebrows, good bust ... Vastly happy with her future expectations ... talks incessantly. No fixed character, a light and flighty mind, but meaning well and well disposed – my eternal theme to her: to think before she speaks, to recollect herself. Flippant, rattling and coarse. Such giddy manners cannot please the prince.
(Assessment of Caroline of Brunswick in 1795 by Prince George IV's friend and confidant James Harris, Earl of Malmesbury)

It was the rise of Southend, coupled with a great dislike for her foppish husband, that gave German-born Caroline Amalie Elisabeth of Brunswick her Essex connection. Born on 17 May 1768, she was the second daughter of Duke Karl II of Brunswick-Wolfenbüttel and his wife Augusta Charlotte, the sister of George III of England. Despite their being first cousins, it was arranged that Caroline would marry the Prince of Wales, essentially to get him out of £630,000 of debt. The Prince's tastes, however, ran more to sophisticated women; at the time of their marriage, he found Caroline immature for her twenty-seven years. For a Prince who valued beauty and grace, he held her to be hideously ugly, referring to her throughout their relationship as, 'short', 'fat', and 'rude'. It also did not help that George was in love with his mistress of ten years, the Catholic Mrs Fitzherbert, to whom he was illegally married. Ironically, it was Mrs Fitzherbert that Prince George sent to receive his future bride on her arrival in England from Brunswick.

The wedding of thirty-two-year-old George, Prince of Wales, and Princess Caroline took place on the evening of 8 April 1795 in the Chapel Royal at St James Palace. Dressed in rich and heavy clothing, including a robe of ermine-lined velvet, she found standing and walking difficult. The groom also found balance an issue as he arrived at the wedding very

Princess Caroline of Brunswick. (*Author's own collection*)

drunk, his attention throughout diverted to his latest mistress, the forty-two-year-old Lady Jersey. The king himself at one point had to urge him into finishing the ceremony.

The wedding night was no better. According to his new wife, George fell down drunk 'under the grate where he fell and where I left him,' thus sleeping the whole night in front of the fire. Their Brighton honeymoon was spent in the company of George's friends in an atmosphere of drunkenness and 'loose morals', with Lady Jersey in attendance as Lady of the Bedchamber to the future queen, a position appointed by the Prince.

Despite all this, a child resulted exactly nine months later on 7 January 1796, but the event heralded an official separation between the Prince and Princess. From that point on, the couple's paths rarely crossed. George's dislike for his wife was such that he denied Caroline any rights to the raising of their daughter Charlotte, leaving the little girl's upbringing to the care of his mother until an auspicious marriage was made for her in 1816. He even wrote up a will, two days after Charlotte's birth, where he announced:

> She who is called the Princess of Wales, the mother of my daughter, should in no way be concerned in the education or care of the child, or have possession of her person ... to my daughter I leave my jewels, which are mine having been bought with my own money – and to her who is called the Princess of Wales I leave one shilling.

After 1798, Caroline set up a separate household in Montague House, Blackheath, and soon gathered a small court around her. Despite this estrangement from her husband, the Princess remained popular with the public. The Prince's expensive habits – which he assumed taxpayers would pay for despite economies imposed upon them to finance the Peninsular Wars – were partly to blame. So, too, was his ongoing relationship with Maria Fitzherbert and at least one other mistress. Caroline's behaviour soon began to reflect her neglect. Constantly without sufficient funds, often socially snubbed and sexually frustrated, her conduct became, to say the least, indiscrete, reckless, and disreputable. It was a popular belief at the time that Caroline was 'a depraved woman but an injured wife'.

Concerned about his wife's increasingly flirtatious manner, George restricted Caroline's visitation rights to their daughter, who as she grew suffered from a painful condition in her knee. Whether Caroline was included in the decision to send the young Princess away for the benefit of her health is not known. At the time, it was believed that sea bathing in one of the new and fashionable resorts could cure most ills. In 1836, a report was made on the medical benefits of bathing in Brighton:

Bathing preserves the softness and flexibility of the skin, contributes to general cleanliness, and consequent comfort, and even to bodily elegance ... Wherever bathing can possibly be procured, provided it agree with the constitution of the individual, it ought to be occasionally used during the greater part of the year; for, although merely an external application, it has often a wonderful influence in the removal of disease, even from some of the most internal organs of the body; and where no disease exists it is useful as a preventive.

But it was not to Brighton that the young Princess was despatched, but to one of the newest sea bathing resorts at the time, Southend-on-Sea.

The five-year-old Charlotte took up residence in the house of Mr Sumner, a relative of the Archbishop of Canterbury, in a house called The Lawn. This was in the tiny hamlet of Southchurch, or Seachurch, a stone's throw from Southend, where even as late as the 1890s the beach walk was described as being no more than a 'cart track, with waving cornfields stretching to the brink of the sea'. Charlotte's health flourished here. Southend, too, had come a long way from the ramshackle dwellings and the singular sea jetty it had once been.

Profitable oyster beds had given John Remnant a reason, in 1767, to build cottages for the oyster fishermen at the 'Southe-end of Prittlewell' parish. The two turnpike roads to London, one through Rochford and the other through Hadleigh, greatly improved a daily coach service. A year later, in 1768, a scheme was put forward to 'render' Southend a convenient place for bathing, 'the situation being esteemed the most agreeable and convenient for the purpose of the Essex coast.' Though this never quite got under way, the landmark Ship Inn was built, and, by 1790, there were nineteen houses in the town, a theatre by 1793, and, by 1795, cold and warm sea water baths were opened.

When she bathed, Charlotte was often attended, it is said, by a Mrs Glasscock, her personal 'dipper'. Charlotte also attended services at Holy Trinity church. Here, the Revd Thomas Archer, curate at Southend and Shoebury, would give his weekly sermons; being a great character as well as a follower of the hunt, he would wear hunting pink under his surplice should a weekday service clash with a hunting appointment. Once engaged in marrying a couple, he broke out with a 'Tally Ho! Tally Ho!' when the hounds were heard to go by.

During August and September 1804, Princess Caroline, not wishing to join her husband's friends and mistresses in Brighton, visited 'New Southend'. Caroline and her small entourage of servants took several houses in the Grand Terrace which, as part of Thomas Holland's vision of Southend as a sea-bathing centre, was built in 1794 on a prominent ridge to the west of the 'Old Town'. A library, assembly, and coffee room soon followed. A visitor at that time described it as being an 'earthly paradise: and I doubt not that South End will be the rage, since even in its infancy nobility has deigned to join the mystic dance, and the loveliest of England's pride to grace the promenade and the terrace.'

Due to Caroline's patronage of the new upper town, the Terrace was renamed 'Royal' soon after her visit. In 1806, *The Globe* newspaper began to publish a list of those in society who visited the new fashionable resort. Such persons were also mentioned in the *Chelmsford Chronicle*. The following is from an article dated Friday, 2 August 1805:

Yesterday Lady Hamilton gave a grand dinner, a ball and supper to the fashionables at Southend to which her Ladyship also invited all the naval officers in or near that place in honour of the Hero of the Nile. Southend is, we understand filling very fast with the most fashionable company the best lodging being for the greater part engaged. The spirit of building has again revived and many improvements have lately been made, the transfer of property at this most delightful spot has of late been very frequent and every circumstance leads to the supposition that houses will become more valuable every year.

It was also about this time that Revd Thomas Archer penned his famous poetical *Description of South End* in which he predicted: 'Til a new South-End in each spectators eye, With Weymouth, Margate and Brighthelmstone vie.'

But, unlike most society ladies, ministerial scrutiny was to follow Caroline everywhere. In an endless quest to be rid of his unsophisticated and ill-educated wife, George had every rumour and scandalous event connected with the Princess investigated. A Royal Commission was established to examine the allegations that Caroline had given birth to an illegitimate child, a claim put forward by a lady-in-waiting, Lady Douglas, but this was disproved by the commission's close investigation in the summer of 1805. It did claim, however, that the Princess had 'romped familiarly' and 'dallied immodestly' with a number of naval officers, and that her conversation was all too frequently 'littered with sexual innuendo'. The details of one particular incident, recounted by one of her servants, concerned a certain Captain Thomas Mamby, master of the fifth-rate frigate, *Africaine*, whom the Princess entertained while on her visit to Southend.

I have several times seen the princess, after having gone to number 7, – we kept in there being the rest of the company, – retire with Captian Mamby from no 7, through to no 8 to no 9 which is the house where the princess

East Parade, Southend-on-Sea (about 1830).

Views of Southend-on-Sea which Princess Caroline would have been familiar with. Royal Terrace, where she took three separate dwellings in 1803 and entertained Captain Manby, can be seen in the distance (top left). (*Bob Nicholls*)

A closer view of Royal Terrace at the top of what is today Pier Hill. (*Bob Nicholls*)

slept. I suspect that Captain Mamby slept very frequently in the house, hints were given by the servants, and I believe that others suspected it as well as myself. Captain Mamby was there three times a week at least while his ship lay for six weeks off Southend at the Nore. He came as tide served in the morning by 10 o'clock I suspected he slept at no 9, the Princesses room, she always put out the candles herself in the Drawing room at no 9 and bid me not to wait to put them out. She gave me the orders as soon as she went to Southend. I used to see water jugs, basins, and towels set out opposite the Princess' door in the passage, never saw them so left in the passage at any other time. And I suspect he was there at that time, there was general suspicion throughout the house.

Unfortunately for Prince George, the 'Delicate Investigation', as the inquisition into Caroline's affairs became known, was not able to provide enough evidence for the Prince to be rid of her. On the contrary, it only lowered his own credibility, the public believing the Princess' lapses in morality were secondary to the Prince's own. His popularity waned as Caroline's increased, so much so that in 1814 the Whig Government demanded that her allowance be increased. To ease the taxpayers' burden, she happily accepted £35,000, though she was offered an annual grant of £50,000. After this grant, she almost immediately left for the continent where she said she hoped she would be able to live with the correct honours due a Princess of Wales.

Caroline, however, was never one for prudence; once abroad she embarked upon an adulterous relationship with Bartolomeo Pergami, an obscure Italian veteran of Napoleon's Russian Campaign. 'Employed' as her secretary, it was he who persuaded her to buy a villa on the shores of Lake Como. From her travels in Italy, Germany, the Greek Islands, Constantinople, Jericho and Jerusalem, it wasn't long before reports of Caroline's behaviour were filtering back to England and scandalizing genteel society. Now approaching fifty and very plump, her behaviour in posing for a portrait with 'her person much exposed', and driving through Genoa in 'a gown that had a low-cut bodice and short white skirt, with a pink hat covered in pink feathers', shocked many back in England.

With Princess Caroline abroad, her daughter Princess Charlotte grew up under the distant but tyrannical rule of her father, who, in 1811, had become Prince Regent due to King George III's decline in health. The Prince's fear that Charlotte would take after her mother prompted him to curtail her social life, vet her friends, constantly threaten to dismiss her women and forbid her to see any member of her mother's rakish court, especially Lord Byron, with whom it was alleged she had, for a short while, been romantically involved.

Charlotte married Prince Leopold of Saxe-Coberg, a happy and affectionate match, but died of complications following the birth of a stillborn child in 1817. The country was genuinely grieved, but it took the Prince Regent's accession to the English throne to finally bring Princess Caroline home. Both Caroline and George knew that his coronation would afford her the title of Queen Consort, and even as Caroline travelled back through Switzerland in May 1819, asking for the royal Yacht to be made ready to meet her at Calais on June 3, George once again demanded a divorce.

Caroline returned home to face a government-prepared 'Bill of Pains and Penalties' that – without resorting to a formal court of law, which might have divulged details of George's own adulterous relationships – set out to deprive Caroline of the title of Queen and declare her marriage to the king 'for ever wholly dissolved, annulled and made void'. The Bill did not succeed and Parliament rather surprisingly granted nearly a quarter of a million pounds for the coronation, service, and festivities. Despite the king's refusal to include her in the forthcoming auspicious occasion, Caroline continued with her preparations for her role as queen by inquiring of Lord Liverpool what 'ladies of high rank' would carry in her train and 'what dress His Majesty would desire her to wear'. Her stubbornness, however, did not gain her entry into Westminster Abbey on 19 July 1821. She was repeatedly refused admission at all the doors, her ensuing demonstrations dismissed as tiresome interruptions by George as he proceeded with the five-hour ceremony.

Caroline died shortly afterwards on the evening of August 7, not of 'humiliation' as thought by some, but from complications following abdominal pains suffered in late July while attending a theatre performance at Drury Lane. To avoid any demonstrations, her initial wish for her body to be taken back to Germany, first on a state barge downriver to the Nore off Southend, then on a warship to Elbe, could not be honoured. The admiralty had no suitable vessel so instead the funeral proceeded through London to Harwich, resulting in several disturbances, and the death of one rioter.

It was no fault of the king. During the week of the funeral, he had behaved with remarkable diplomacy. It was his wife's popularity, and the inscription 'Caroline of Brunswick, the injured Queen of England' that she had insisted be engraved on her coffin, that was to ensure George remained forever callous in the eyes of history.

3

WIVES

ADAM'S RIB

She was a mother as wise as she was fruitful.

(Bridget Peck memorial)

According to the writer Daniel Defoe, it was not unusual for women living in villages and on remote farms in Essex to find themselves a fifth, sixth or even seventh wife of an Essex man, his former wives having died. In his journal *A tour thro' the Whole Island of Great Britain*, published between 1724 and 1727, Defoe describes 'Essex Fever', also known as the 'Marsh Ague', a malady that was responsible for many female deaths. Women born and bred on the marshes and coastal inlets were effectively immune to what was actually malaria, but women from inland Essex taken as wives by the men from these areas were not. Defoe describes it thus:

I have one remark more, before I leave this damp part of the world, and which I cannot omit on the women's account; namely, that I took notice of a strange decay of the sex here; insomuch, that all along this county it was very frequent to meet with men that had had from five or six, to fourteen or fifteen wives; nay, and some more; and I was inform'd that in the marshes on the other side the river over-against Candy Island there was a farmer, who was then living with the five and twentieth wife, and that his son who was but about 35 years old, had already had about fourteen; indeed this part of the story, I only had by report, tho' from good hands too; but the other is well known, and easie to be inquired in to, about Fobbing, Curringham, Thundersley, Benfleet, Prittlewell, Wakering, Great Stambridge, Cricksea, Burnham, Dengi, and other towns of the like situation: The reason, as a merry fellow told me, who said he had had about a dozen and half of wives, (tho' I found afterwards he fibb'd a little) was this; That they being bred in the marshes themselves, and season'd to the place, did pretty well with it; but that they always went up into the hilly country, or to speak their own language into the uplands for a wife: That when they took the young lasses out of the wholesome and fresh air, they were healthy, fresh and clear, and well; but when they came out of their native air into the marshes among the fogs and damps, there they presently chang'd their complexion, got an ague or two, and seldom held it above half a year, or a year at most; and then, said he, we go to the uplands again, and fetch another; so that marrying of wives was reckon'd a kind of good farm to them: It is true, the fellow told this in a kind of drollery, and mirth; but the fact, for all that, is certainly true; and that they have abundance of wives by that very means: Nor is it less true, that the inhabitants in these places do not hold it out; as in other countries, and as first you seldom meet with very antient people among the poor, as in other places we do, so, take it one with another, not one half of the inhabitants are natives of the place; but such as from other countries, or in other parts of this county settle here for the advantage of good farms; for which I appeal to any impartial enquiry, having myself examin'd into it critically in several places.

No statistical evidence in the form of burial records bear out this supposed imbalance of men to women, but historian Philip Benton reported that an epitaph on a gravestone in St Mary's churchyard, South Benfleet, could just be testament to Defoe's observations.

> Sixty-three years our hoyman sail'd merrily round,
> Fourty-four liv'd parishioner where he's Aground,
> Five wife's bear him thirty-three children Enough;
> Land another as honest before he gets off.

Of course, another reason for a high female mortality rate was the high death toll in childbirth. Difficult deliveries could not be eased as they are today. Doctors were expensive and medicine was selective.

The obstetric forceps were invented by Peter Chamberlain of Woodham Mortimer in the seventeenth century. Chamberlain's early forceps were modelled on midwife's spoons and were known to have been straight instead of curved. They were made of either wood or steel, and padded with leather. Today, correctly applied, the use of forceps is safe, offering protection as well as assisting in the extraction of the child during a difficult labour. Despite resembling instruments of medieval torture, Chamberlain's invention was effective.

However, this lifesaving invention hardly helped matters for ordinary women. Chamberlain kept it a closely guarded secret, only available to wealthy women who could pay handsomely. He made sure his invention arrived at a confinement in a gilded box, and that the lady in question was blindfolded; he was not prepared to rely on the prudery of the times which dictated that medical administration should be conducted under the bedclothes to preserve a lady's modesty. Such was Chamberlain's pride and greed that, when he died in 1683, his invention died with him. Ordinary women continued to die of complications; not until the beginning of the eighteenth century did one of Chamberlain's descendants finally free the obstetrical forceps for general use. After decades of gathering dust, many original instruments were discovered under the floorboards in the attic of his home in 1813. His widow, no doubt at his request, had hidden, among other things, the obstetric forceps in various stages of development.

Countless infant deaths would have been avoided had Chamberlain not kept his invention a secret, but childbirth had always been a dangerous time for women. As the time for birth drew nearer, it was not unusual for a woman to set aside the clothing she would be buried in should she 'die in childbed'. At the same time she made provision for the child's layette and her own 'lying in'.

There was little comfort for men who lost their wives this way, even less if the child died too. A grieving husband could do no more than pay tribute to his dear wife's virtue on her tombstone. On a plaque in Little Baddow chapel is a poem describing William Parry's sorrow at the death of his thirty-one-year-old wife, Rachel, and two of his children within months of each other in 1791.

> Insatiate Archer! Could not one suffice? Thy Shaft flew thrice and thrice
> my Peace was slayn. And thrice, ere thrice yon Moon had fill'd her Horn.

His anguish is made all the more poignant as he was Pastor there from 1780 to 1799.

Margaretting's small church with its shingled spire contains a tombstone inscription of 1666 to the devoted married couple Peter and Julian Whitecoombs:

> She on this clayen pillow layd her head
> As brides do use the first to go to bed
> He missed her soone, and yet 10 months he trys
> To live apart, and likes it not, and dies...

Another example of exulted womanhood can be found in the Church of St Mary the Virgin on the crossroads to Thaxted and Saffron Walden. Here the lady in question is Bridgit Peck. Carved in marble above her sarcophagus, she reclines on cushions, an open book in her left hand, her long hair curling over her shoulder as she dreams into the future. She was obviously much loved by her husband, for his tribute celebrates, among other things, her abundant fruitfulness which saw her bear him eight daughters and two sons before she died aged 31. This is a translation of the Latin inscription:

> Enshrined beneath this marble monument lie the mortal remains, to wit the beauty, grace and form most elegant, noble and virtuous, of Bridget, an excellent and singular example of womanhood. Her husband was William Peck, her father Morgan Randyll, both knights. The latter of Chillworth in the district of Surrey, the former of Samford Hall in the County of Essex. To them, while she survived, had been an exquisite ornament and delight, now alas long deceas'd. A woeful loss and cause for universal tears! Yet if her obsequies must be perform'd with grief her thousand (nay more!) pleasing virtues destin'd for an eternal existence will be rehears'd on the lips of all to whose their report has come, or some day yet shall come. She was in deed endow'd as if by heaven itself. Gifts most agreeably compos'd for the fulfilment to ev'ry duty, be it to God or neighbour or herself, who was daughter, spouse, parent, matron, and all these to an excellent degree. She had, o marvel, a disposition without guile or subterfuge and what rarer to be found in the weaker sex, marvelous fortitude, which she display'd as often as some matter required. In shaping the character of her offspring, she was a mother as wise as she was fruitful (indeed at her decease she left two sons and eight daughters) and to this task she exercised herself with no little a success which, had time allowed, would have become greater still. In these pursuits engaged, neither desirous nor yet fearful of the grave, only ripened for heaven and observant of its councils, being 31 years of age, she died on the 14th day of June in the year of our Lord 1712. That this monument should be forever sacred to the matchless virtues of this cherished form was the wish of her most afflicted spouse.

Praise indeed, but it does raise the delicate question that perhaps his love for his lady may have had something to do with her demise. For many a modern woman, such 'fruitfulness' suggests she may well have died of exhaustion!

As in everything, there are exceptions to the rule. Many documents in Essex show women also outliving their husbands. Mucking church has on its monument to Dame Elizabeth Downes, who died in 1667: 'she lived happily with four husbands'. Martha Blewitt of Birdbrook, who was buried on 7 May 1681, obviously found marriage to her liking as on a commemorative tablet in the parish church it states she was 'ye wife of nyne husbands successively, buried eight of ym, but last of all ye woman dyed alsoe'. In 1690, a woman referred to simply as 'the widow Raven' was buried on 12 January being 'above 100 years old'. In St Clement's chuchyard, Leigh-on-Sea, beneath the 'cutlass stone' (so called because men of the press gang supposedly sharpened their cutlasses upon the tombstone while waiting for the men of the village to emerge from church on a Sunday morning) lies Mary Ellis, daughter of Thomas and Lydia Ellis, who, as 'a virgin of virtuous courage and promising hope', died in 1609 aged 119 years old.

As individual common women had far less written about them than their wealthier sisters, sometimes they come to our attention simply for the peculiarity of their names. For example, the daughter of Richard Springham, a gentleman mercer of London, was also the wife of Richard Bristow Esq. of Pitsey (Pitsea) for twenty-six years. When she died on 20 January 1611, aged fifty-five, she was remarkable purely for having been

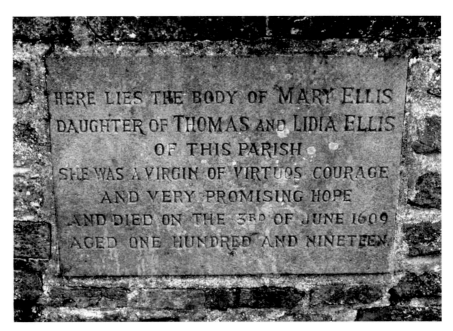

An exception to the rule: Mary Ellis of Leigh-on-Sea lived to a ripe old age, the inscription suggesting that she was born at the end of the fifteenth century and died in the early years of the seventeenth century. Her tomb immediately outside the church door is topped with a huge flagstone with deep grooves in it, locally known as the 'Cutlass Stone'. Legend has it that this was where the press gangs would wait on a Sunday morning for the local men to leave church so that they could press them into the navy. While waiting, it is said they sharpened their cutlasses upon the tomb to pass the time.

given the outstanding name of Mercymight! In 1666, Bowers Gifford buried a lady called Prudentia Love. A will, again from Pitsey, dated 1692 concerns the goods and chattels of a widow with the wonderful if strange name of Frizwith Dore, while a will from Shalford, proved in 1699, cites the lady's name as Damaris Lukin. Charity Marchand was an Essex woman living in Ardleigh in 1786, and a Bathsheba Smith was baptised on 18 May 1788 in Stock. Essex's strong Puritan heritage lasted well into later centuries with Silence Law being born at White Colne in 1823, and Jerusha Rambert born the daughter of a thatcher from Tendring in 1861.

We cannot, in a book about Essex women, overlook that most 'Essex' of women's names – Mehala. Often thought to have been introduced to the county by the writings of Sabine Baring-Gould, Rector of Mersea from 1871 to 1881, it appears that the name of his feisty eponymous heroine was certainly in circulation in Essex as early as 1769, when Mehala Whipp was born in Harwich. The name definitely featured in parish registers and census returns before his book, *Mehalah – A Tale of the Salt Marshes*, was published in 1880. Perhaps Baring-Gould took the name from Mehala Moss, born in Steeple in 1807. He could equally have been inspired by Mehala Benning, born in Halstead in 1874, or from any one of the women christened with that evocative name before 1880.

THE DISTINGUISHED DAUGHTERS OF GIDEA HALL (1524–1610)

The industry of the females was in full vigour.

The four daughters of Lady Ann and Sir Anthony Cooke of Gidea Hall were a phenomenon in their day. At the time, girls were rarely educated, being groomed instead to be good wives. But Sir Anthony, the tutor of King Edward VI, was a great believer in the freedom education could give an individual. He engaged tutors for his own children, and made sure that his daughters benefited from the same levels of teaching as his four sons. Languages were taught, both ancient and modern, while mathematics shared importance with sciences and astronomy. Many books were read and great debates on religion were undertaken. Such was the girls' contribution that the scholar Walter Haddon (1515–1557) commented on the Cooke household at Gidea Hall in an oration to the University of Cambridge:

The four daughters of Sir Anthony Cooke of Gidea Hall and Lady Ann, his wife. Each daughter was exceptionally well educated and they were married into some of the leading families of the day. Lady Mildred became the wife of Sir William Cecil, the Lord High Treasurer of England and privy councillor to Elizabeth I. Ann married Sir Nicholas Bacon, Keeper of Elizabeth I's Great Seal. Elizabeth married first Sir Thomas Hoby, the Queen's Ambassador to the French Court, and then married John, Lord Russell. Katherine married the most accomplished of Queen Elizabeth's diplomats, Sir Henry Killigrew.

And what a house did I find there, yea, rather a small university, in truth while staying there I seemed to be living in a Tusculan villa, except only that in this Tusculum, the industry of the females was in full vigour.

Mildred, Sir Anthony and Lady Ann's eldest daughter, was born in 1526. At the age of twenty-two she became the wife of Sir William Cecil, the great Lord Burleigh, Lord High Treasurer of England and Privy Councillor to Elizabeth I. She excelled in Greek and was said not only to be a scholar, but as good a politician as her husband. She was exceedingly benevolent, but her charities were as secret as her generosity. Four times a year she 'relieved' poor parishioners in London. She also left legacies; one of £120 – a vast sum in those days – was to be lent without interest to six needy tradesmen in Romford.

Sir Anthony's second daughter, Ann, was born in 1528. Another distinguished scholar, she married Sir Nicholas Bacon, Keeper of Elizabeth I's Great Seal. Her 'piety', it was said, 'was as deep as her learning was profound'. She and her husband often entertained the queen. She was also the mother of Francis Bacon, whom the queen referred to as 'my young Lord Keeper' on her visits when he was a boy.

Sir Antony's third daughter, Elizabeth, born 1529, was no less distinguished. Her first husband, Sir Thomas Hoby, was the queen's Ambassador to the French Court, where he and Elizabeth lived. They had three children together before he died. One of Elizabeth's sons by him became the Speaker of the House of Commons. Another, born just after her husband's death, was named Thomas Postumous. Elizabeth returned to England and later married John, Lord Russell, who, when he died, was commemorated with a grand monument in Westminster Abbey.

Katherine, Sir Antony's fourth daughter, followed in her sisters' footsteps. Proficient in languages including Hebrew, she was also a poetess and married the most accomplished of Queen Elizabeth's diplomats, Sir Henry Killigrew.

Keeping a watchful and learned eye over all her daughters was Lady Ann, daughter of Sir William Fitzwilliam of Gains Park in Theydon Garnon, Essex. A strong woman herself, she had made Gidea Hall her home on her marriage; it became the nursery of one of the most gifted families in the land.

It was Sir Anthony Cooke's dearest wish that when his daughters married they should find 'complete men' and, in turn, the men they chose to marry found happiness and companionship with 'complete women'. He was more than successful. His daughters were educated enough to be any gentleman's equal, but gracious enough to let their husbands think otherwise.

DOROTHY BASSET (1528–1603)

To own a fortune has always made a woman a very valuable commodity. Widows, once released from both a father's and late husband's control, enjoyed the management of their own affairs perhaps for the first time, and could enter the marriage market again, but this time with a degree of choice. However, to inherit an estate on the death of your father and still be under age often meant you had no choice at all. Lady Dorothy Basset was one such Essex girl, but one who was later to prove she definitely had a mind of her own.

When Dorothy's father, Gregory Basset of Bassets Hall, died in 1528, Dorothy was only a year old. As she was under the age of inheritance – fourteen for a girl and twenty-one for a boy – Dorothy became a 'ward' and the Basset estate in Great Chishill, which was in Essex until county boundaries changed in 1895, reverted to the crown. This ancient practice had brought in an income for the monarchy since Anglo Saxon times and was a safeguard against historically diminishing land holdings of the tenant-in-chief. As a consequence, it meant that Dorothy's marriage rights also became the property of the monarch. But complications arising from the administration of this cumbersome medieval system meant that wardships were not kept in Crown hands for long, and nearly always went up for sale. If lucky, a subject could find their wardship sold to the next of kin. If not, as another lucrative form of revenue for the crown, it was simply sold to the highest bidder.

As a widow and not an heiress in her own right, Dorothy's mother Margaret seems to have had little or no say in this arrangement. She received, by law, only one third of her husband's estate and so possibly did not have enough funds to keep herself as well as buy back her daughter's legal rights, as would have been required of her. Dorothy quite possibly continued to live with her mother as she grew up, though wardship included providing an education for the ward and, in some instances, required the subject to be schooled elsewhere or indeed reside with his or her benefactor. Had Margaret, at a later date, wanted to claim back her daughter's wardship, it was, unfortunately, no longer to be had. It had been 'obtained' by Thomas Bonham of Stanway, Colchester, while she was still an infant, and he was determined to retain it. As 'King's Receiver' with goods assessed at over £200 in both 1524 and 1525, Bonham was by no means a poor man. Nor was he to be thwarted. An expert in manipulating the system, Thomas Bonham had every intention of being as successful at collecting wards as he was in collecting Colchester's taxes.

The extent of Bonham's determination to ensure his own children married well and for profit is evident in a transcript of his will, dated

Then and now: Saling Hall, the home of Lady Dorothy Basset, has changed little over the centuries. (above, *author's own collection*; below, *Robert Hallmann*)

1532. Firstly, he instructs his wife to 'support his four sons until they come of age', then he sets out his instructions as to whom they are to marry:

> To son William the farm that I have of Sir Thomas Tey knight in Peldon, co. Essex and that he be married to Francis Tey one of the daughters and hiers apparent ...
> Son Walter to be married to Alice Dale 'my warde' if they agree ...
> Son Henry to be married to Margaret Adell 'my warde' if they agree ...

Bonham not only provided eligible partners with valuable estates for his sons, but the will goes on to mention his daughters Elizabeth and Anne, one of whom had already married John Barrington. When, in a different document, it states that John Barrington 'married the daughter of his guardian Thomas Bonham, and his wife Catherine, sister and heir of Henry Lord Marney, Knight of the Garter,' it becomes quite clear that Thomas Bonham was ensuring his family climbed the social ladder on the backs of other people's fortunes.

Thomas Bonham's will also dictates that his fourth son Robert 'be married to Dorothy Basset 'my warde' if they shall come to agree'. We have no date for the marriage between Dorothy Basset and Robert Bonham, but one can assume it was not long after she came into her inheritance at around fourteen. It is also rather doubtful that there was much 'agreement' about it. This is borne out by the fact that when Dorothy married her second husband in 1548 she was already the mother of at least four children and hardly more than twenty-one years old.

Having been dominated by her husband and trapped in childbirth up to that point, Robert Bonham's early death suddenly released Dorothy from all Bonham control. For the first time in her life she was free to make her own choice and take charge of her own affairs, which she did with a will. Consequently, she rid herself of the family which had effectively bought her as a child. She reverted back to her maiden name – something unheard of in those times – and married again, disowning the children of her childhood marriage. The man of her choice was Anthony Maxey of Saling Hall, a judge and an Essex man of some standing. She also foiled Thomas Bonham's master plan when she took her inheritance with her. In fact, the couple set up home on her property of Bradwell Hall, near Coggeshall. Unfortunately, history portrays Dorothy as a callous woman with a heart of stone, yet she must have thought of herself as nothing short of an oppressed captive to make so bold a stand.

Dorothy Basset's marriage to Anthony Maxey lasted for forty years. Dutifully, she produced another six children: three sons and three daughters. Both a son, Anthony, and a daughter, Jane, died young, but

Dorothy Basset became Dorothy Bonham when she entered into a forced marriage around the age of fifteen. She died as Dorothy Babington in 1603, but it is as Dorothy Maxey that she wished to be remembered. She lies buried beside Anthony Maxey, her second husband, in the family church of Bradwell-juxta-Coggeshall; her likeness is captured in an alabaster effigy kneeling upon their tomb. Theirs was a love match that lasted for forty years. (*Robert Hallmann*)

of the remaining two daughters from this second union, Bridget married Edward Wentworth of Bocking Hall, and Dorothy married to Sir Edward Heron, one of the Barons of the Exchequer. Both made good marriages, as did her sons Henry and William, who both emulated their father and became judges, and, unlike their father, achieved knighthood. William married Helena, daughter of Sir Edward 'Grevyle', while Henry, the eldest, brought the Maxey family close to royalty by marrying Myldred, a daughter of William Cooke of Gidea Hall. Her mother was Frances, daughter of Lord John Grey, and therefore cousin of the ill-fated Lady Jane Grey.

Alas, Henry died childless, but William went on to provide Dorothy with ten grandchildren, seven girls and three boys. William brought his children up to fear God and honour the King; he got them up 'by five of ye cloc in the morning' to demand his blessing and, once given, a recitation of the Lord's Prayer and various chapters of the bible. A Royalist family, Dorothy's three grandsons, Grevil, Henry and William, certainly embraced the Crown and rose to high office in the Royalist army; William even fought for Charles I at the siege of Colchester in 1648 as Major General of the King's Horse, at a time when Essex was a staunch Puritan stronghold.

Although Dorothy settled her inheritance upon her second family, it may be fair to say that she was not as heartless as some historians would have us believe, and it could be argued she never really left her children from her first marriage. As there is scant information on him, it can only be assumed that her firstborn son Charles died, but to her second son Jerome (Jeremy), Dorothy and Anthony left an annuity of £10. In Jerome's will, dated 1630, he speaks of his 'loving mother' and my 'well beloved brother Henry Maxey'. Possibly ill from childhood, he bequeathed money to the servants of the Maxey household for their services to him and speaks only of his 'room', which suggests he may well have been living with the Maxeys at the time of his death. He also refers frequently to his nephews and nieces, making clear that his sisters had married well enough while he himself appears not to have married or had children of his own. The fact that he bequeaths only his bible, a chest, tools and money for a feather bed to be 'bought in his honour' suggest he was certainly not a man of property.

Dorothy did marry again when Anthony died, aged sixty-seven, in 1590. Perhaps she, at the age of sixty-two, was looking for companionship in her latter years. Born Dorothy Basset, she died Dorothy Babington in 1603, but it was as Dorothy Maxey that she wished to be remembered. She lies buried beside Anthony Maxey in the family church of Bradwell-juxta-Coggeshall, where, above the altar in an ostentatious monument that partly obscures the east window, there is an alabaster effigy of her kneeling with her second husband Anthony and her childless second son Henry and his wife Myldred. On the alter tablet is written:

The said Sr Henry married Myldred one of ye daughters of Willi'm Cooke, esq 2 son of Sr Anthony Cooke of Gyddy Hall in ye Countie of Essex knight, by Francis his wife daughter of ye Lord John Gray, brother to Henry Lord Gray Duke of Suffolke both sones of Thomas Marques Dorset Lord Gray of Grooby, which said Sr Henry Maxey in reverent memory of his said parents hath erexted this monument.

PENELOPE DEVEREUX (1563–1607)

Outstanding in beauty, gifted in every quality of mind and body.
                                                    (Robert Johnston, historian)

An 'Essex girl' by marriage and association, sister to the volatile Earl of Essex, Penelope Devereux managed to exchange a disastrous arranged marriage to a dour, puritanical, if 'rich', husband, for a dashing soldier, administrator, courtier and expert jouster in the tilt-yards. She also became the muse of one of the greatest Elizabethan poets of the time.

In an age of female subservience Penelope Devereux refused to be suppressed. Her strength of character was tested many times, most notably when she was implicated and interrogated for her supposed part in her brother's uprising against Queen Elizabeth. Her superior intellect allowed her to manipulate most situations to her advantage. With the Elizabethan spirit of vitality and adventure almost exclusively embodied in the great men of the day, Penelope possessed a confidence that made her their equal.

Perhaps Penelope was too beautiful to be left unmarried for long. Born in 1563, she was almost eighteen when she first attended Court and made an impression upon the matchmakers, whose job it was to arrange the right marriage often for the wrong reasons. Yet they had not been the first to encounter her dangerous beauty. Prior to her arrival at Court, she had been betrothed to Philip Sidney, an engagement that had come to nothing due to Philip's desire for adventure, a decision he grew to bitterly regret.

Penelope and Philip first met when she was thirteen years old. Reputedly, he was part of the royal hunting party that visited her father's half timbered, gabled house in the ruins of Old Chartley Castle in Staffordshire. A four year betrothal followed, during which time Penelope, already a good singer and dancer, perfected her skills on the lute, became literate in French and Spanish, and charmed all who knew her with her 'fineness of wit'. With her father, Sir Walter Devereux, the Earl of Essex, being a military man and a courtier, and her mother, Lettice Knollys, a granddaughter of Mary Boleyn, Penelope was a desirable catch for any young man. That Elizabeth I was her Godmother only added to the heady mix.

The Sidney marriage did not take place for a variety of reasons, one of them being Sidney's lust for adventure. On his death, Penelope's father had left her a handsome dowry of £2000, plus £100 a year. This financially embarrassed the Sidneys; due to their heavy investment in the Irish wars, they were in no position to provide their son with the means by which he could set up his own establishment and provide for a wife. Another reason was that old Sir Henry Sidney realised that he no longer had to nurture the fragile and uneasy friendship that existed between the two families for political reasons. Another possibility may be that Penelope and Sidney were no longer, or never had been, truly in love. It took Penelope's appearance at Court as one of Queen Elizabeth's ladies-in-waiting and as another man's wife – namely Lady Riche (Rich) – for Sidney to lament what he had lost.

Penelope had not so much lamented the marriage that had been arranged for her, but had protested most strongly against it. It was rumoured that she complained bitterly, even at the altar, stamping her feet and refusing to cooperate, causing her uncle to take her aside and tell her that she would be turned out penniless into the street if she did not accept. A document in the British Library, though written long after the event, appears to verify this. 'A lady of great birth and virtue, being in the power of her friends, was by them married against her will unto one against whom she did protest at the very solemnity and ever after.' Had her father lived he might not have sanctioned the match. But marriage to the young and eligible Robert Riche, who had just succeeded to a title and considerable property, was financially advantageous to others as well as Penelope. On All Hallows Eve, 1 November 1581, the strikingly dark eyed Penelope Devereux married a churlish and uncouth member of the Essex gentry.

The wedding was an important event, but as the queen's court were preparing for the arrival of the Duke of Anjou in London, the aging Elizabeth's prospective suitor (she was now forty-six), it was a little overshadowed. Nevertheless, there was feasting, singing and dancing, despite Lord Riche's puritanical aversion to such things. The young couple received some lavish wedding gifts; Penelope received a silver cup from Lord Roger North costing the princely sum of £11 16s, far more than what his New Year's present to the queen had amounted to.

After her wedding, home for Penelope was Leeze (also Leez and Leighs) Priory, a fine mansion tucked away to the east of Chelmsford on the banks of the river Ter. The imposing house had once been a monastery, founded by Sir Ralph Gernon in 1220. It had been 'acquired' by her husband's grandfather, the scheming Richard Riche, whose management and manipulation of the Dissolution of the Monasteries in the late 1530s saw him rise from lawyer to 'new money' landowner. To make way for her new daughter-in-law, the dowager Lady Riche had moved out of Leeze and resettled at Rochford Hall, another family property, thus enabling Penelope to preside over her new matrimonial home

Seldom, if ever, did Penelope speak well of her husband. Robert Riche, by all accounts, was not a pleasant man. Possessing a foul temper, he was both uncouth and vindictive. In one instance he chose to deny a lifetime tenancy granted to one of his park keepers, William White, something

Lady Penelope Riche at Lambeth Palace. On the reverse is written, 'A Countess of Devonshire'.

which had been upheld by both his father and grandfather. As his men had besieged the cottage for a week, effectively starving White and his family out of their home, Riche found himself brought before the Sheriff of Essex. For endangering the lives of his tenants he was found 'uncharitable' and strongly advised to put the case before a proper court of law, and never again to take matters into his own hands.

Despite this, Riche became a Justice of the Peace, not on merit, but because he was a baron. His name appears on most of the local assize records of the time. This did not mean that he was competent or at all popular. In 1582, the vicar of Felsted bitterly complained that Riche had, in a fit of pique, deprived him of Rayleigh, one of the benefices granted to him by Riche's own grandfather, a living he had held along with Felsted for twenty-four years. His tirade went on to state that 'there were none of Lord Riche's neighbours but would be glad if he were further from them'. Also, Riche was not above insisting that men be brought before him for misdemeanors that had already been discharged by a higher authority.

With his manners as rough as his conversation, Riche knew he appeared dull and uneducated in the light of his wife's accomplishments, yet he recognised Penelope's influence in places and situations where he had none. Just before their marriage, when he had been brought before the Bishop of London's court over a religious matter, it had been Penelope's position at Court that was his saving grace, securing him no more than a severe reprimand. From that point on, he was always to show her a grudging respect.

Penelope, by contrast, found she could not respect a man she did not love or even like. When Riche accompanied her brother Essex to Cadiz, he was noted by his absence when there was fighting to be done. When, he volunteered for an expedition to the Azores, he had to be put ashore suffering from seasickness. In a letter to the queen, Essex had mentioned disparagingly that if he insisted Riche 'let him carry him to sea', he would have been dead in a week.

It is an understatement to suggest that Penelope found life at Leeze difficult. Having experienced a strict northern upbringing, she had wholeheartedly embraced life at Court and was not about to accept Riche's regime of nightly prayers, or his ideal of a subservient wife. As this demanded that she be 'humble, sober and silent, never quarrel, to stay at home when her husband was away, be merry when he was merry and sad when he was sad, take neither strong drink or delicate food, undertake to be a good housekeeper, show loyalty and never to cross him instead to persuade him with wise advice', Penelope could not help but disappoint her husband.

Continuing as lady-in-waiting to the queen, she found she could divide her time between her position at Court and her wifely duties, or as many as she was prepared to undertake at Leeze. Still not yet twenty she found a friend again in Philip Sidney, in whose company she could forget that she was married. A love affair began and Sidney found himself writing of her constantly in his poetry. His most famous work *Astrophel and Stella* was, by his own admission, largely autobiographical; the part of the lover, Astrophel, was the personification of his feelings towards Penelope. References to the identity of this woman of undeniable beauty and 'richness of spirit' are hinted at in many of the poem's sonnets. In sonnet thirty-seven, Sidney makes it plain who Stella really is with a pun on Penelope's married name: 'she hath no misfortune, but that Riche she is'.

The affair was brief and ended in the summer of 1582 when Sidney retired to his father's estates in Herefordshire. He married Frances, the daughter of Lord Walsingham, in 1583, a choice that seems to have been an especially happy one. Drawing on her strength of spirit, Penelope resigned herself to her husband and their life in Essex, but she made sure it was a life over which she would have full control. After her interlude with Sidney, she became a mother. Her first two children were girls. The first she called Lettice (Lucy), after her mother, and the second was named Essex after her father. On 19 March 1587, she gave birth to Robert, an heir for Riche, named not so much after her husband as for her beloved brother, who was rapidly becoming Queen Elizabeth's favourite. There followed another daughter in 1588 who died soon afterwards. A second son, Henry, was baptised on 19 August 1590, and was her last child by her husband.

Penelope's children were *'her Richest jewels'*, and as a loving mother they were a great source of pride to her. It was for them that she schemed and planned the family's advancement, her husband, by contrast, preferring to bury himself in local Essex affairs. To best serve her children's interests, Penelope continued to attend the queen, though she frequently returned to Leeze to act for, and assist, her husband in matters concerning the estate. It soon became apparent, however, that it was not just the queen who was getting her attention at Court. Almost nine years after she had married Robert Riche against her will, Penelope Devereux had become the mistress of Charles Blount, Lord Mountjoy.

Mountjoy was everything Riche was not. When he was seen wearing Lady Riche's colours at the tournament held in November 1590, in honour of the queen's accession day, it was taken by all to be a public indication of their feelings for one another. It was also reflected in the lines of a poem written by George Peele to commemorate the royal occasion:

> Comes Sir Charles Blount ...
> Riche in his colours, Richer in his thoughts,
> Riche in his fortune, honour, arms and art.

Robert Riche did not challenge this relationship. Not the sort of man to demand satisfaction in a duel, his protests took the form of snide comments and petulance that did nothing for his standing amongst his peers. He also knew that to cast her out would alienate him from her influential brother, the Earl of Essex (1566-1601), a move he was reluctant to make. Instead he tolerated the situation, even giving his name and a home to the children his wife had produced with Charles Mountjoy, allowing them to be brought up amid his own. Contrary to the popular belief that the two families at one time overlapped, Robert Riche's second son was not Mountjoy's child. Proof now exists that Penelope and Charles's first baby, a daughter called Penelope, was born in 1592, two years later than originally thought, thus securing Riche as the father of Henry, baptised in 1590. Once Penelope had fallen in love with Mountjoy, she would not entertain the continuation of her marital duty towards her husband. Robert Riche's divorce statement, dated 15 November 1605, corroborates this, as he admits that all physical relations had ceased between him and Lady Riche after her affair with Mountjoy had become public. Speaking of his wife, Riche reveals that he 'had not for the space of twelve years enjoyed her'.

From this point on, Penelope split her time between Leeze Priory and Essex House, the home of her brother, having apartments there in which she and Mountjoy enjoyed each others' company, and where some of her children were born. Amazingly, the life she now led did not affect her or Mountjoy's standing at Court. In fact, by having the courage to leave her unhappy marriage, she was able to move about 'in a man's worlde' with a degree of independence unknown to most women of her time. She still returned home if her husband requested it, especially when he was ill as she was legally bound to do so.

Mountjoy, once committed to Penelope, was utterly faithful, considering her his wife in all but name. She, in turn, bore him three sons, Mountjoy, Charles and St John, and two daughters, Penelope and Isabella. All children received the surname Riche. Another son, Scipio, died soon after birth in 1597, possibly due to the fact that while she was carrying him Penelope contracted smallpox. It was rumoured that she had been greatly disfigured by the disease, but it later became known that 'lady Riche is recovered of her smallpox without blemish to her beautiful face'.

As the decade drew to a close, Lady Riche's concerns for her brother Robert were to bring out in her qualities of loyalty, resourcefulness, bravery and intelligence that would put her own life in danger. Essex was rapidly falling from grace. He had, from boyhood, amassed serious debts, upward of £30,000, and now, having seriously displeased Elizabeth by disobeying her orders during his Irish campaign, had been imprisoned on his return in 1599. Falling seriously ill, he had asked his sister for help. Penelope spent many hours at Court pleading his cause, even dressing in mourning black to bring attention to his plight. Disillusioned with Robert Devereux, the queen finally distanced herself from her former favourite and would not allow Penelope access to her brother despite him at one instance being close to death. Penelope renewed her efforts to secure her brother's release by writing impassioned letters to the queen in words carefully chosen to point out that her brother had been conspired against and that in time those conspirators might turn against the throne itself.

Penelope was ordered to Leeze, under her husband's control, until called back to London to appear before the Privy Council and account for herself. Not one to be intimidated, Penelope showed great courage before her interrogators and eventually was released with only a serious reprimand from the queen. Almost immediately, she found herself back at Leeze nursing her husband who was 'extream sick'. As soon as he was improved, she returned to London to find her brother released but rounding up supporters for a rebellion to help him save the queen from what he considered were traitors in her court.

When the rebellion failed, Essex was once more arrested and at his trial he ungallantly implicated Penelope in the plot he had hatched. This time Penelope was put on trial. Having been betrayed by her brother, abandoned by her husband, and without Mountjoy, who, at the queen's command, was in Ireland putting down the uprisings that had cost Essex his reputation, she was alone, but showed great strength and courage in the face of death.

Never did she say anything that could incriminate the brother she loved. She showed incredible resolution and eventually managed to convince the queen of her loyalty. Her brother was not so fortunate. He was executed, still protesting his devotion to the queen, on 25 February 1601.

Not having had the courage to divorce his wife while her influential brother was still alive, Robert Riche now filed for divorce. Penelope co-operated with her husband to obtain their separation citing her adultery with a 'stranger' rather than dragging her lover's name through the courts. Now aged forty, Penelope found herself a free woman, but both she and her former husband were instructed by the judges, to live chastely and celibately and forbidden to re-marry 'while the other is alive'. Penelope and Charles Mountjoy cemented their long relationship with a wedding ceremony on 26 December 1605, performed by William Laud at Wanstead House, believing that should they offend the courts they would be liable for the payment of a substantial fine at most. But the benevolent Elizabethan era had passed, and it was no longer deemed acceptable for divorced couples to remarry. Two years into the reign of James I, the laws surrounding marriage had taken a puritanical turn and a charge of bigamy could be applied to a person who remarried while their former partner was still alive. Mountjoy appealed to the king, justifying the marriage for the sake of his new wife and children, but James I was adamant the marriage was invalid, telling Mountjoy: 'You have won a fair woman with a black heart.'

It is thought that the disgrace heaped upon the couple as a consequence of their marriage contributed to the Earl's untimely death only three months after the wedding. Mountjoy's funeral as the Earl of Devonshire was conducted with the pomp and ceremony befitting a man who had served his country well, but when his coat of arms was presented during the proceedings, Penelope's heraldic emblems had not been included. Further indignities were to be heaped upon Penelope. With her marriage invalid she was no longer recognised as the Countess of Devonshire, the title she had held as Mountjoy's wife, and was further humiliated in certain circles by being referred to as Lady Riche. Determined never to be known by the name she detested, she chose to be known simply as the Lady Penelope, preferring to have no surname at all. Penelope was also called to account for the generous provision made by the Earl, in his will, for her and her children. Accusing her of knowing the union was illegal when Laud had married the couple, lawyers insisted the Earl had made the will knowingly fraudulent.

With customary resilience, Penelope defended herself against those that accused her of fraud and corruption and those that called her a harlot and a mercenary. But the strain took its toll on her health. She had taken the death of her husband, Mountjoy, badly, 'laying utterly dejected in a corner of the bedroom for a night and a day in mourning' according to contemporary historian Robert Johnston, writing in Latin fifty years later. In July 1607, she contracted a fever and died aged only forty-four.

Robert Riche duly waited until marrying again as decreed by his divorce, though whether he did so 'chastely and celibately' is questionable. In 1618, the year of his death, Riche bought a title from King James I for £10,000. Riche, then the Earl of Warwick, was buried in Felsted.

As at the time of her death, Penelope belonged to neither the Riche nor the Blount families, and where she was buried remained a mystery for a long time. Matters were made worse by the age of Puritanism that tried hard to obliterate all traces of the beautiful temptress with the golden hair and defiant dark eyes. But now it is thought that she lies alone, interred at All Hallows church, Barking, by the Tower of London, recorded in the unpublished registers as simply 'A Lady Devereux'.

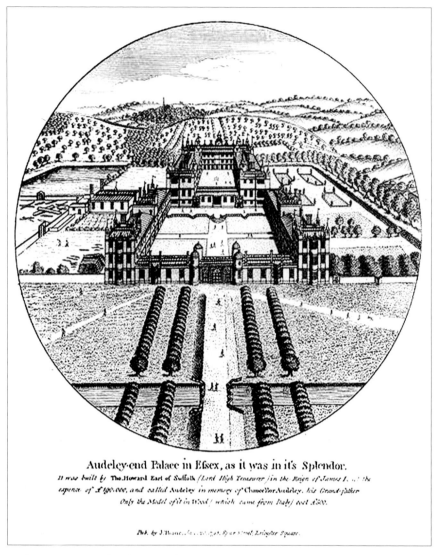

Audeley-end Palace in Essex, as it was in it's Splendor.

It was built by Tho. Howard Earl of Suffolk (Lord High Treasurer) in the Reign of James I. at the expence of £190,000, and called Audeley in memory of Chancellor Audeley, his Grand-father. Only the Model of it in Wood, which came from Italy cost £500.

Pub. by J. Thane...

Katherine Knyvet's first home with her husband was Audley Inn, but she soon influenced her husband to demolish it and rebuild Audley End House in its place. This picture shows it in 'all its splendour', having been built at a cost of £200,000. (*Robert Hallmann*)

KATHERINE KNYVET (1564–1633)

As with Elizabeth Cromwell, one thing that most Essex women had in common were children. It was a woman's lot to produce them, and if a woman was married, whether through choice or duty, having children was hard to avoid. Contraception was crude, if used at all, and consisted mainly of potions (the condom, or sheath, was not introduced into England until the eighteenth century). Women relied on folklore or other women at these times, often going to great lengths to no avail; in many cases a particular mixture of herbs and spices was used to promote conception or to abort pregnancies. The juice of the herb savin, nicknamed 'cover-shame', was a known 'restorative of slender shapes and tender reputations'. Marjoram, thyme, parsley, lavender, and bracken were also supposed to be a preventative, as were certain powders in warm ale. Even the humble honeysuckle would prevent pregnancy if drunk by a husband or lover for thirty days, as this was supposed to render him 'unable to beget any more children'.

Had they fully realised it, women who breastfed their own children unwittingly indulged in a natural form of birth control; generally, a woman's fertility is suppressed until her child is weaned. But rich women almost exclusively employed a wet nurse and in doing so condemned

Audley End as it today. Although a third of its former size, it is still imposing, the front elevation having been built up over the centuries. (*Robert Hallmann*)

themselves to having very large families. Their poorer sisters, by performing this service, had on average fewer children, often able to limit their children to only half a dozen instead of twice as many. Katherine Knyvet (or Knivet) had thirteen children. Yet this formidable woman still found time to involve herself in the duplicitous world of Tudor politics.

Katherine was the daughter of Sir Henry Knyvet of Charlton and Elizabeth Stumpe, and stepsister to Sir Thomas Knyvet, the man who foiled the Gunpowder Plot in 1605. She was a celebrated beauty of her time and though not strictly born an Essex woman she became one twice, through marriage, firstly to the Honourable Richard Riche, son of Robert, 2nd Baron Riche, and then to Thomas Howard, 1st Earl of Suffolk, sometime before 1583.

Katherine was only nineteen when she married for the second time, and her home became Audley Inn, the former Walden Abbey granted to Sir Thomas Audley by Henry VIII at the Dissolution of the Monasteries in 1538. The building had been converted into a domestic mansion and served the family well until 1603, when it was demolished on the orders of Katherine's husband and replaced with the palatial house named Audley End, that stands today outside Saffron Walden. If Katherine had urged her husband to improve upon the family's residence in order to better entertain King James, it is not known, but confidence in her own beauty had made Katherine bold and manipulative; when the mansion was finished in 1614 it included a suite of rooms for both the king and queen. It is also reported to have cost £200,000, which Thomas Howard told the king on his first visit to the house. Suitably impressed, James I is reported to have commented that 'the building is too large for a King but it might do for a Lord Treasurer', the post Thomas Howard had been awarded the year the house was finished.

As both the wife of the Lord Treasurer and Countess Suffolk, Katherine enjoyed an elevated position at Court. Despite providing the Howard dynasty with many children, she undoubtedly found time to use her position to her and her husband's advantage. Perhaps she had a hand getting her husband appointed as Lord Treasurer. That she had a hand in his downfall is certain. In 1618, grave irregularities were found in the Treasury and Thomas Howard was suspended from the office he had held for four years. He was charged with embezzlement, defrauding the king and extorting money from the king's subjects, while Catherine, through her friendship with Sir John Bingly, Remembrancer of the Exchequer, was accused of using this lucrative relationship to enrich herself.

Both Katherine and her husband were imprisoned in the Tower and in danger of execution. Both were held for extortion, but, when Katherine was interrogated by the Court of the Star Chamber, it transpired that she had also been in the employ of Spain and was receiving £1000 a month to act as a spy.

The couple escaped drastic retribution from the king, though they were only released from their imprisonment after those they had cheated were reimbursed and a hefty fine had been paid to the Crown. They returned in disgrace to Audley End; public opinion of the time accused Katherine of being to blame for the whole sordid affair. Eight years later, Thomas Howard died aged sixty-six.

As she saw it, Katherine's life was cut short too. Though she lived another seven years, her remarkable beauty, even at the age of fifty-five, had deserted her soon after her public humiliation. In 1619, an attack of smallpox 'spoiled that good face of hers, which had brought to others much misery and to herself greatness which ended with much unhappiness'.

Left with massive debts and nine surviving children, this wife, mother, schemer and unlikely spy died in 1633, aged sixty-nine.

ALICE AND GRACE MILDMAY
(1588–1615 & 1552–1620)

Grace approached medical care in a logical manner, dealing first with anatomy, then the types of available drugs, then the preparation of medicines ... and finally the causes and treatment of diverse diseases.
(Lady Grace Mildmay)

Of the two women connected with the Mildmay family of Essex, Lady Alice Mildmay, who died in 1615, is the most renowned. It is she who is said to haunt the mile-long avenue of trees, known as 'Grace's walk', which leads up to 'Great Grace's Farm' the medieval mansion house once inhabited by the Norman 'Le Gras' family, after whom it is named. It is she who reputedly drowned herself in a pond at the place where Graces' Walk crosses Sandon Brook, after her husband, Sir Henry Mildmay, to whom she was a child bride, was supposedly unkind to her. The story is thought to be more fiction than fact. More likely it was a tale invented or embellished by Jesse Berridge, the Rector of Little Baddow from 1915–1947, to help publicise a novel he had written.

By comparison, it is Lady Grace Mildmay who really deserves our attention. Born Grace Sharington in 1552, she grew up a Protestant at a time when most of England was still Catholic. Her home was Lacock Abbey, bought from the Crown by her father after the Dissolution for £738. Here, with her sisters Ursula and Olive, she enjoyed a life of privilege, yet deep down she doubted she deserved her good fortune. When

Grace's Walk where, it is alleged, Alice the young wife of Sir Henry Mildmay took her own life rather than continue in a loveless marriage. (*Robert Hallmann*)

the monasteries, the chief centers of charity, had been abolished by Henry VIII, care of the sick and the poor fell naturally to those who had acquired church lands. Lady Grace Mildmay was one of the first women to take up these duties and provide any sort of medical help for those in distress.

A medical practitioner at a time when women weren't considered equal to men, she spent her time administering to those in need on her husband's lands in both Northamptonshire and Essex. While she did not perform surgery, she did study the latest medical books and made her own medicines using local herbs and exotic imported products such as tobacco. In many ways she was a product of Elizabethan society, yet in others she pushed the boundaries of accepted sixteenth-century womanhood. She has left memoirs of her extraordinary life, detailing her thoughts on parenthood, on her husband Anthony Mildmay, and what she thought of her father-in-law Sir Walter Mildmay, Chancellor to Queen Elizabeth I.

She also leaves us with insights into how homes should be governed and servants regulated, especially warning 'daughters' against listening to the serving men of the household, 'whose ribald talk and idle gestures and evil suggestions were dangerous to chaste ears and eyes to hear and behold'. But perhaps her most glorious gift to the future was her 250 different works on diseases, medicines and treatments.

As with all brides, Grace had hoped for happiness in her marriage, but her union with Anthony Mildmay was not a love match. 'I carried always that reverent respect towards him', she declared in 1617 after fifty years of marriage, 'and for that I could not find it in my heart to challenge him for the worst word or deed which ever he offered me in all his life.'
Duty, as well as the times she lived in, prevented her from defending herself against her husband's ignoble tongue, and it was her faith that consoled her throughout those barren circumstances. Hers was a strong religious conviction. It had been especially tested by her father on his deathbed, when he left her almost penniless, at the behest of her mother and sister, to encourage her to trust in God.

Medicine became the passion of her life and she spent a huge percentage of her meagre income on medications to treat those in need who called upon her. To put Grace's finances into context, she can be compared to another noblewoman, Margaret Gwynnethe, who as a silk-woman at the Court of Henry VIII was in the service of both Anne Boleyn and Catherine Parr. After her death on 16 September 1544, her husband wrote to a court official asking for the £360 that Catherine Parr owed Margaret for her materials and labour. In 1544, that was an enormous sum and needless to say he was a long time in being paid. A few years later, Lady Grace Mildmay was maintaining her family on only £130 a year.

Had she lived today, Grace would have been eligible for a university education. But in her day such formal education was denied women; instead, those in positions of privilege were expected to use their natural talents to be useful. Grace, however, read everything she could get her hands on concerning medical matters, including an English translation of a book by Jean de Vigo on surgery. Under the deep-seated belief at the time that medicine worked ultimately under the umbrella of 'God's will', she made treatments for jaundice, skin diseases, cramp, ulcers, memory loss, fevers, eye problems and melancholy. Even the 'falling down sickness' (epilepsy) was cured in a maid of twenty-five with a balming oil for her ears and a herbal drink made of eringo roots as a 'mollification of the symptomatic convulsions'. This remedy was taken every day for three years after which Lady Mildmay rejoiced that 'she finally became free from that disease, thanks be to our Lord Jesus Christ'. Despite being a talented physician, Lady Mildmay's modesty meant she would not take full credit for her remedies, believing instead that her faith in God and his divine providence was what ultimately made those remedies work.

The writings Lady Grace Mildmay left behind her cannot help but convey her sense of continuity, of forward thinking. Containing advice and guidance as well as medicines and remedies, her works were aimed largely at her grandchildren and were illustrated by personal examples; she truly believed they would transcend the restricted conditions of her own lifespan. 'All these things coming into my mind, I thought good to set them down unto my daughter and her children, as familiar talk and communication with them, I being dead, as if I were alive'.

One of Grace Mildmay's favourite treatments was a balm that she made herself, containing '24 types of roots, 68 kinds of herbs, 14 types of seeds, 12 sorts of flowers, 10 kinds of spices, 20 types of gum, 6 different purgatives, 5 different cordials'. Note the heating method – stand 6 days in horse dung!

A most precious and excellent balm.

Roots:
acorns or great galingale 1 ounce, 6d; peony root 1 ounce, 3d; angelica root 1 ounce, 4d; iris 1 ounce. 1d; cormeskill root 1 ounce, 2d; enula campana 1 ounce, 1d; citron rundes & co. 2 ounces, 2s; foleroots 1 ounce, 2d; liquorice 1 ounce, 1/2d; marshmallow roots 1 ounce, 1 1/2d; the bark of caper root 1 ounce, 3d; the inner bark of tamarisk 1 ounce, 4d; saxifrage root 1 ounce, 4d; filipendula root 1 ounce, 3d; resta bovis 1 ounce, 2d; aristolochia rotunda 1 ounce, 4d; male valerian root 1 ounce, 4d; bistort root, 1 ounce, 2d; gentian 1 ounce, 4d; red dock root 1 ounce, 1/2d; fennel root, 1 ounce, 1/2d; chicory root 1 ounce, 1/2d; setwall root 1 ounce, 6d; wild dragon root 1 ounce, 3d.

Herbs:
sage 1 handful, 1d; betony 1 handful, 1d; sweet marjoram 1 handful, 6d; rue 1 handful, 1d; wild thyme 1 handful, 1 1/2d; eyebright 1 handful, 2d; fennel 1 handful, 1d; vervain 1 handful, 1d; balm scordion 2 handfuls, 6d; cardus benedictus 2 handfuls, 2 1/2d; scabious 1 handful, 1d; bugloss 1 handful, 1d; borage 1 handful, 1d; St John's wort 1 handful, 1d; isop folefoot 1 handful, 1d; maidenhair 1 handful, 4d; wormwood 1 handful, 1d; germander 1 handful, 1d; enula campana 1 handful, [no price]; agrimony 1 handful, 2d; chicory and sowthistle 1 handful, 1d; plus sticados and elder tops, 1 handful each [no price]; monseare 1 handful, 2d; plantain 1 handful, 1d; ceterach 1 handful, 4d; hart's-tongue 1 handful, 4d; sowbegrass 1 handful, 1 1/2d; finiterry 1 handful, 1d; speedwell 1

handful, 1d; golden wand or virga aurea 1 handful, 4d; yarrow 1 handful.
1d; knot-grass 1 handful, 1d; pellitory-of-the-wall 1 handful, 2d; mugwort
1 handful, 1d; nep, featherfew, smallage 1 handful, 1d; camapiteos 1
handful, 1 1/2d; mercury 1 handful, 1 1/2d; langue-de-boeuf 1 handful,
1/2d; bugle 1 handful, 2d; pimpernel 1 handful, 2d; cinquefoil 1 handful,
1 1/2d; parsley 1 handful, 1/2d; clove 1 handful, 1 1/2d; sothernwood 1
handful, 1 1/2d; avyns 1 handful, 1 1/2d; chickweed 1 handful, 1 1/2d;
camomile 1 handful, 1 1/2d; lavender 1 handful, 2d; express 1 handful,
[no price]; savory 1 handful, 1 1/2d; lavender-cotton 1 handful, 1 1/2d;
burnet 1 handful, 2d; rosemary 1 handful, [no price]; mallows 1 handful,
1/2d; strawberry leaves 1 handful, 1d; tansy 1 handful, 1 1/2d; pennyroyal
1 handful. 1d; filipendula 1 handful, 1 1/2d; endive 1 handful, 1d; dill 1
handful, 1d; maudlin 1 handful, 1d; saxifrage 1 handful, 1 1/2d; horehound
1 handful, 1d; oculus 1 handful, 1d; orris 1 handful, 1d; red and damask
roses 2 ounces, 7d; brook thyme 1 handful, 1d.

Seeds:
lovage 1 ounce, 4d; peony 1 ounce, 2d; aniseeds 2 ounces, 2d; sweet
fennel 2 ounces, 4d; basil 1 ounce, 3d; violet 1 ounce, [no price]; plantain
1 ounce, 2d; alkekengie berries 3 ounces, 3 1/2d; cormwell 3 ounces, 1d;
citron 6 ounces, 9d; sorrel 6 ounces, 2d; mather root 3 ounces, 2d; siler
montanum 2 ounces, 1d; nigella romana 2 ounces, 1d.

Flowers:
rosemary 1 handful, 10d; sage 1 handful, [no price]; betony 1 handful, 4d;
red jelevers 1 handful, 12d; marigold 1 handful, 4d; violet 1 handful, 6d;
chicory 1 handful, [no price]; tamarisk 1 handful, 6d; camomile 1 handful,
2d; cowslips 1 handful, 3d; borage 1 handful, 6d; bugloss 1 handful, 6d.

Spices:
cloves 1 ounce, 8d; nutmeg 1 ounce, 6d; ginger 1 ounce, 2d; grains 1 ounce,
2d; cubebs 1 ounce, 20d; cardamoms 1 ounce, 6d; galingale 1 ounce, 8d;
cinnamon 1 ounce, 8d; maces 1 ounce, 10d; pepper 1 ounce, 4d.

Gums:
salbam 1 ounce, 4d; ammoniac 1 ounce, 6d; mastic 1 ounce, 10d; myrrh 1
ounce, 16d; adellin 1 ounce, 10d; storax calamita 1 ounce, 12d; spikenard
1 ounce, 20d; caraboe 1 ounce, 8d; tragacanth 1 ounce, 4d; segapinum 1
ounce, 6d; opoponax 1 ounce, 30d; benzoin 1 ounce, 24d; venis turpentine
4 ounces, 12d; sebestens 3 ounces, 10d; junibes 2 ounces, 6d; pine kernels
1 ounce, 4d; saffron 1 handful, 14d; ambergris 1 scruple [no price]; musk
1 scruple, 30d; gum traback [no price]; sack of the strongest 6 gallons,

16s; strong white wine vinegar 2 pints, 12d; oil olive of the best 2 gallons, 6s; sugar of the finest 6 pounds, 7s; Jordan almonds 2 lbs, 2s.

Purgatives:
rhubarb fine 6 ounces, 60s; aloes fine 6 ounces, 6s; agaric fine 6 ounces, 9s; hermodactiles 4 ounces, 6d; turbith fine 4 ounces, 4s; sene alex 4 ounces, 1d.

Cordials:
diacurcumen 2 ounces, 6s 8d; diamuskadneses 2 ounces, 8s; diarrhodonebatus 2 ounces, 6s 8d; diatrionsantalon 2 ounces, 6s 8d; nia entrand, 28s
Sum Total £10 10s.

The making of the said balm:
Take all the aforesaid herbs and roots and infuse them in the wine vinegar and oil in a vessel close stopped. And 2 or 3 times a day shake or stir them together and so to stand infused 6 days or the longer the better in horse dung (if you will) or otherwise. Then put all the aforesaid in a body with a limbeck and distil it over, drawing the water from it only, for the oil must remain in the bottom with the herbs. Then put back the water again and let them infuse as before, shaking them together twice or thrice a day. And then distil again as before until 3 times it be distilled over. Then strain it hard and wring all substance from the herbs and then cast away the herbs.

And then put in your spices and gums, infusing them and shaking or stirring them together as before, until the same have been distilled 5 or 6 times over or until small quantities of the water will arise in the stilling, provided that the oil remains on the bottom with the spices as before. And then strain it and wring out hard all substance from the fleece and wash away all the oil clean from the fleece with some of the water.

Then put in your cordials and purgatives, using them in the like manner as before is specified. Then let it stand and settle until it be cold and then with a spoon skim off the oil and reserve it in a glass.

Then boil the residue which remaineth or evapour away the liquid substance and so reserve it as a precious extraction of this balm to be used many ways outward and inward or as iriithridatum with some unicorn horn, bezoar stone or for what other purpose you will. You may make it agreeable for every purpose provided that the aforesaid cordial and purgatives be first prepared with the strongest aqua vitae 4 times distilled before they be put unto the oil and balm, with some other observations as we know.

ELIZABETH CROMWELL (1598–1665)

Dearer to me than any creature; let that suffice.

(Oliver Cromwell)

It is not immediately obvious that Elizabeth, the wife of one of England's most famous – or infamous – sons, started life as an Essex girl. Her marriage in London at St Giles' church, Cripplegate and her subsequent homes in Cambridgeshire seem to place her firmly out of the county. Yet it was almost certainly here along the low and windswept fringe of southeast Essex that she became acquainted with the young Oliver Cromwell. Later, her four sons attended school at Felsted.

Elizabeth was the eldest of the twelve children, nine sons and three daughters, born to Sir James Bourchier and his wife Frances Crane. Sir James had inherited land and property from his father, and was himself a successful London businessman, thought to have been involved in the fur and leather trades. Knighted by James I in July 1603, he also owned property around Tower Hill in the City, and lands in Essex, including Little Stambridge Hall.

Elizabeth grew up enjoying the privileges that her father's status afforded her and it's possible she became acquainted with the young Oliver Cromwell through Essex social circles. As with any love story, romantic theories abound. One suggests the couple met through family ties, which later acquainted Oliver with some of the leading Puritans in the country. Another is that Oliver fell in love with the daughter of the house when he and his friend, the son of the Earl of Warwick, rode out from Rochford Hall, a stone's throw from Little Stambridge, to visit Elizabeth's brother. If they did meet this way, and Oliver courted Elizabeth beside the creeks and quiet lanes around her home, it would have been ironic indeed. For the man history remembers as the killer of a king was walking in the footsteps of one of England's greatest monarchs. A hundred years before, Henry VIII, the man who thought nothing of executing his queens, may have amorously pursued his lady of Rochford, Anne Boleyn, in the very same way.

There is no picture or genuine description of Sir James Bourchier's eldest daughter, but it's known that the young Elizabeth was two years older than Oliver Cromwell when they married in 1620. The marriage proved to be a long and stable one, in which Elizabeth lived happily in her husband's shadow. For this reason little is known about her character except that she was literate and level-headed enough not to be at all phased by her husband's years as Lord Protector of England, especially during their years at Whitehall. This made her a target for Royalist propaganda. By comparing her mercilessly with the vivacious Queen Henrietta, she

Elizabeth Cromwell, painted by Sir Peter Lely. Elizabeth grew up enjoying
the privileges that her father's status afforded her, and it's possible she became
acquainted with the young Oliver Cromwell through Essex social circles when living
at Little Stambridge Hall. (*The Cromwell Museum*)

was derided for being a plain housewife. She was called dull and dour. In scandalous pamphlets she was unflatteringly referred to as 'Protectress Joan' (a common servant's name); her thrifty nature was despised as that of a miserly woman who kept her husband's table short of food and denied him comfort.

In truth, Elizabeth was a modest woman and, far from denying him comfort, provided her husband with 'benefit of the bed' to the tune of seven children in the first decade of their marriage. Obviously a fertile lady, the gap of five years before Elizabeth had her last two children could have been down to unrecorded miscarriages or, as some modern scholars have dared to think, a conscious form of family planning. A more likely theory points to a downturn in family fortunes during the years 1631–35. This saw Cromwell sell nearly all his property around Huntingdon and lease a farmstead at St Ives, where he worked as a farmer for five years. James, the couple's last and youngest son, also died in this period soon after his birth.

Elizabeth and Oliver's situation improved in January 1636 when, as beneficiaries of a relative's will, the couple were left property and businesses in and around Ely. Soon the Cromwells were living in a comfortable house not far from the cathedral, and by the late 1630s they were among the wealthiest inhabitants of the town. With family status and prosperity restored, Elizabeth found herself pregnant with their eighth child and soon after, her ninth. Elizabeth was an able teacher to all her children but later, as they grew older, her sons attended Felsted school. Sadly her eldest son, Robert, died of smallpox there in 1639, aged only eighteen.

Elizabeth's marriage was a strong one, surviving the strain of her husband's frequent absences while he was on military campaigns. The few surviving letters between the couple reveal a deep and enduring affection, if a little measured on Oliver's part. In one letter to his wife, Cromwell declares her to be 'dearer to me than any creature; let that suffice'. He continues: 'My Dearest, I could not satisfy myself to omit this post, although I have not much to write; yet indeed I love to write to my dear, who is very much in my heart.' In her one surviving letter to him, written in December 1650, Elizabeth expresses a desire to see her husband again, and admits: 'Truly my lif is but half a lif in your abseinse'.

As Cromwell's influence throughout the country grew, their union also survived scurrilous attacks upon Elizabeth's reputation. By 1650, Royalist gossipmongers had sunk to a new low in their scathing attacks. In a pamphlet called *News from the new Exchange* they published the obscene claim that she 'hath run through the most of the regiment, both officers and soldiers'.

Even after Oliver's death in 1658, Elizabeth was fair game for adverse public opinion. One publication entitled *The Court and Kitchin of Elizabeth*

Wife of Oliver Cromwell was written by Randal Taylor six years after Oliver Cromwell's death, with the express intention of further blackening the Cromwell name. Many were unhappy with the fact that Elizabeth and her family were allowed to escape retribution after her husband's death and England's grisly revenge upon his body (he was exhumed and his head was displayed on a pike on London Bridge). Randall's booklet attacked her mercilessly, accusing her of giving herself airs and deriding her for being 'such a person durst presume to take upon herself such a sovereign estate when she was a hundred times fitter for a barn than a palace.'

In his book, he made public the household accounts of the Lord Protector's time in power at Whitehall. He decried Elizabeth's housekeeping referring to her 'sordid frugality and thrifty baseness', which he said had her running her own dairy and 'pasturing cows in St James' Park' in order to save money. The booklet also featured many recipes, taken from cookery books, and 'volumes of receipts' Elizabeth had produced in her own right. These he used to discredit her further by showing that the food she gave her family was 'ordinary and vulgar, except some few rarities'. In reality it was ill health that prevented Oliver Cromwell from indulging in rich foods. He did drink liberally on occasion to 'void the gravel in his kidneys', which suggests he suffered from kidney stones. Still, the diet Elizabeth provided for her husband was ridiculed as 'spare' and 'curious' and at times when the family went without food Randall had people thinking it was due to Elizabeth's neglect as opposed to the family fasting for religious reasons.

Today, *The Court and Kitchin of Elizabeth Wife of Oliver Cromwell* serves as a tribute to Elizabeth and is a unique collection of recipes from a surprising quarter. Inside we are instructed 'How to make Marrow Pudding', 'Dress Udders and Tongues', 'Stew a Carp' and 'Boil Flounders or Jacks ... after the best manner'. As it was never envisaged that we in the twenty-first century would ever know exactly how our forefathers lived, we are privileged to get such a glimpse of seventeenth-century culinary arts.

At least three of Elizabeth's sons followed their father's footsteps into politics and the Civil War. Oliver and Henry joined the army, but Oliver was killed. Richard, the eldest surviving son, reluctantly succeeded his father to the position of Lord Protector, albeit only for a year. His clumsiness and general lack of competence led him to be nicknamed Tumbledown Dick.

That Elizabeth ended her days in relative obscurity tells us that she was not self-absorbed or filled with any delusions of grandeur. Perhaps her character was shaped by the remote yet resolute Essex landscape that surrounded her growing up in the tiny village of Little Stambridge.

4

WANTONS & MISTRESSES

ELIZABETH 'BESSIE' BLOUNT (c.1502–1540)

She was thought for her rare ornaments of nature and education to be the beauty and mistress-piece of her time.

(Lord Herbert of Cherbury)

Bessie Blount's association with this county may have been short-lived, but it was certainly memorable. At 'Jericho' Priory in Blackmore, about four miles from Brentwood, she gave birth to a king's son; since then, her name has been forever remembered as the mother of the only illegitimate child Henry VIII ever acknowledged. Largely known by her 'pet' name Bessie, it is easy to think of her as a country girl seduced by a monarch who was difficult to refuse. However, she was in fact a member of the gentry, the daughter of Sir John Blount of Kinlet, Shropshire, and his wife Dame Katherine, herself an heiress.

Elizabeth had been familiar with the royal household since childhood. Her mother served as a lady-in-waiting to both Elizabeth of York, wife and queen of Henry VII, and the seventeen-year-old Catherine of Aragon, when she and the fifteen-year-old Arthur, Prince of Wales, had taken up residence at Ludlow, not far from Kinlet, following their marriage in 1501. Close relatives, namely the Blounts and the Crofts, were held in high regard at the Ludlow court; after Arthur's death in 1502, those that returned to London with the Spanish Princess soon rose to prominent positions once she became Henry VIII's queen. It was the influence of one such kinsman, Lord Mountjoy, Queen Catherine's Chamberlain, that gave young Elizabeth her first place in the royal household. On 8 May 1513, her first year's wages were recorded in the 'King's Book of Payments', but as they were not part of the regular wage list it seems that, at that time, her place at Court was not fully established. Twelve years was the minimum age a girl was accepted as a 'maid of honour'; Elizabeth was younger than this which is why she only received one hundred shillings, half the usual rate for such a position.

Even at a young age, Elizabeth was outstanding. Lively and beautiful with fair hair and blue eyes, she was well versed in Latin and poetry and equally good at singing, dancing and 'all goodly pastimes'. She blossomed at Court. Rumours abounded that even at the tender age of fourteen she was already involved with the king. But it was Henry's love of revels and court pastimes that was bringing them together. In a Masque Ball held at Christmas 1514, Elizabeth outshone all other ladies in a dress of 'white satin with mantles of blue velvet and coifs and fillets of damask gold'. On many occasions throughout the evening, the king himself was her dancing partner. Henry had certainly noticed Elizabeth by July 1515. Around this time her father began to reap the rewards of having a daughter at Court; he received a two-year salary advance of £146 as a 'Kings Spear', a royal bodyguard. By now it was evident that Elizabeth had at least 'wan the kings harte'.

Her affair with the king did not take place until after Henry had 'dallied' with several other women throughout his wife's many unsuccessful pregnancies, among them her friend Elizabeth Bryan and a lady several years older than herself, Jane Poppincourt. By the time Henry was ready to seduce Elizabeth, she was a respectable eighteen years old.

Henry's relationship with Elizabeth was no threat to the royal marriage. On 18 February 1516, the queen had given birth to a healthy daughter, the Princess Mary, and so revived Henry's hopes for an heir. 'By God's grace boys will follow!' Henry was heard to declare, and Catherine was pregnant again by 1518. Mindful of the Church's dim view of sex in pregnancy and the fragile nature of his wife's confinements, Henry turned to Elizabeth when he sought the comforts of a woman.

It was a liaison that was not intended to last, but Elizabeth, obviously attracted to the handsome and athletic twenty-six-year-old king, fell pregnant. Women in those days were often in doubt of their condition until the child actually moved in the womb, but as Elizabeth's last appearance at Court was for the celebrations at York Palace to mark the betrothal of Henry's daughter, the two-year-old Princess Mary, to the Dauphin of France, it is likely that she was carrying Henry's child by October 1518.

Henry charged Cardinal Wolsey, his chief minister, with the arrangements for Elizabeth's confinement. As Wolsey's own mistress had provided him with an illegitimate son and daughter of his own, Henry was confident he could rely on his discretion. Wolsey's choice for Elizabeth was the Priory of St Lawrence at Blackmore, near Chelmsford. In opting for a monastery over a nunnery, he was able to stem the tide of gossip that certainly would have flowed had Elizabeth spent her confinement alongside nuns, themselves so often the daughters of the nobility. Here, in the company of monks, Elizabeth resided in the manor house set aside for the Prior, Thomas Goodwyn, and awaited the arrival of her child. In stark contrast to the stillborn girl Queen Catherine had delivered on 9 November 1518, Elizabeth gave birth eight months later to a 'goodly manne child, in beautie like to his father and the mother'. Overjoyed, Henry spent most of the summer of 1519 in Essex.

Certain now he could father a healthy male heir, Henry acknowledged the child and nominated Wolsey to be his godfather. Proud of his achievement, Henry did not conceal the boy but named him Henry Fitzroy – son of the king – a tradition followed by Charles II over a century later. With the birth of a boy proving that Henry could still secure the monarchy

Elizabeth 'Bessie' Blount (later Lady Tailbois), one-time mistress of Henry VIII and the mother of Henry Fitzroy, the King's son. She continued a distant but genuine friendship with the King throughout her lifetime.

for the Tudor line, it is quite possible that the king celebrated his son with the court and household in attendance on him that summer, possibly at his Essex Palace of Newhall at Boreham. It would have been unlikely that even Henry would have been thoughtless enough to share his joy with his queen, who was in residence at her manor of Havering-atte-Bower at the time.

The relationship between Henry and Elizabeth Blount, however, had come to an end. Replaced in Henry's affections by Mary Boleyn, Elizabeth did not return to Court. By 1522, Wolsey arranged for her to be married off to Gilbert Tailbois who, having been swiftly made a knight, was made sheriff of Lincolnshire. As Lady Tailbois, Elizabeth went on to have two more sons and a daughter. By her second husband, Edward Fiennes Clinton, she had another three girls.

Elizabeth remained a stunning woman throughout her life. In 1532, when a staunch supporter of Anne Boleyn was asked to compare Elizabeth with his mistress, he had to admit Elizabeth was the 'most beautiful'. Twenty years later, the king's cousin Lord Leonard Grey declared he had 'had very good cheer' when visiting Elizabeth in Lincolnshire. Henry himself had kept a watchful eye on Elizabeth's welfare through Wolsey.

Of all Henry VIII's mistresses, Bessie Blount, despite succumbing to a king's attentions, has never been regarded by history as a 'loose' woman.

MARGERY HAWLES AND THE PROBLEM OF BASTARDY

Today there is less stigma attached to having a child out of wedlock but in the past it was a punishable offence. Fatherless children today are supported by the welfare state, but in days gone by they were a huge burden on the parish, and great efforts were put into returning a mother and her child to the said parish if she had given birth away from home. In most cases, social and ecclesiastic disapproval was enough, brought to bear in the form of a 'penance' usually performed by the woman when she was 'churched' and welcomed back into a congregation after childbirth. But for some, punishment could be very harsh indeed, as was the case for Margery Hawles.

In an Essex Midsummer Sessions Roll dated 22 May 1589, Justices of the Peace Israel Amyce and Anthony Maxey Esq., the latter of Danbury, found Margery Hawles to be a woman of 'lewde behaviour'. For the crime of being delivered of a child 'unlawfully begotten' she was punished accordingly. These men, as her judges, recommended she be given over to the constables of Halstead who would strip her to the waist, and whip

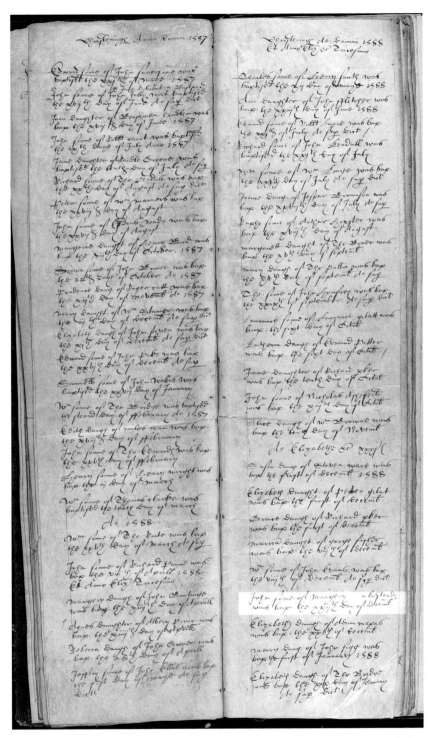

A page from the Earles Colne Parish Register, dated 1588. Near the bottom of the right-hand page is the entry for Margery Hawles' child. (*Essex Record Office*)

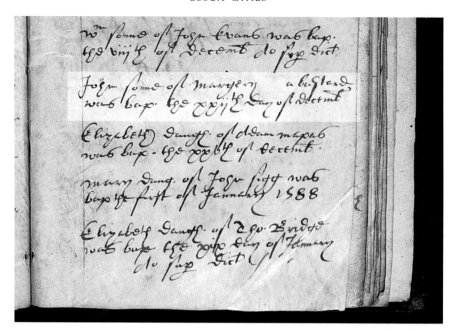

Section of the register clearly showing that 'John sonne of Margery' was entered as a 'bastard'. (*Essex Record Office*)

her while she was tied to the tail of a cart. The sentence was to be carried out openly in the market place the very next day on 23 May 1589, one hour before noon. They decreed that she should suffer twenty-two stripes, leisurely inflicted 'upon her naked body' to serve as an example to other offenders. After her ordeal she was to be freed with the proviso that she was to find work within the next forty days at her peril.

The identity of the father in this case was not known, but until one could be found, her former master, a yeoman called John Stebbing of Stambourne, was to be held responsible. He was required to pay the parish of Earls Colne for keeping Margery's bastard son, called John Hawles, until he reached the age of fourteen. It was, however, written into the judgement that this was only until 'a more likelier man' could be found.

For Margery Hawles, a public flogging was indeed a harsh consequence of having a baby, especially as it appears the father in question suffered no ill effects. But this Essex girl's story is a convoluted tale.

At Margery's examination, William Rust, a clerk, told how he had been employed by Margery's present mistress to confirm suspicions that her servant girl was pregnant. Margery had confessed to him that it was her former master John Stebbing of Stambourne who had got her pregnant, adding she would die if she were lying. Rust swore Margery had told him this six months previously. Another witness swore that John Stebbing

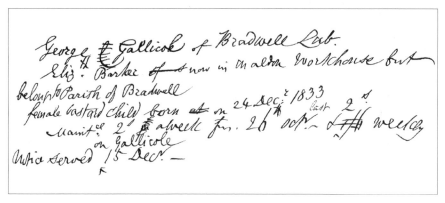

An example of the preliminary details taken by the parish constables for a bastardy order. (*Essex Record Office*)

himself had boasted that he had lain with Margery Hawles 'thrise in one night'.

The court then heard how three female witnesses, one being the midwife who tended Margery in the time 'of her travail', demanded that Margery tell them the true name of the father. Being in the pain of childbirth, Margery still insisted it was John Stebbing of Stambourne, her late master, 'and no other's but his'.

At this point, Margery's examiner called her a 'graceless and faithless wench' for seducing her former master in his own house and with his wife not far away. In her defence, Margery insisted that John Stebbing had been pursuing her for more than a year and in order to have his way with her he had also told her that his wife did not have long to live and that after her death he would marry her.

Whether the father or not, John Stebbing had clearly been involved with Margery. Her sister testified that John had come to her house to visit Margery, after the Braintree fair, and had offered to pay Margery four shillings. He also promised to pay any charges incurred should she know of a place where she could be well looked after and that, when the child was born, he would take it away.

She also said that some days later they had all met in a meadow in Toppesfield parish where John had taken Margery by the hand, confessed that he had indeed known her carnally but 'utterly denied' he was the father of her child. He also said that had Margery told him she was pregnant before it had become common knowledge, he would have provided for her welfare and kept her condition a secret.

John Stebbing twice more offered money in order to be absolved of blame: twenty nobles, approximately £16, to John Blithe, Margery's father-in-law, and £5 to Margery herself, again offering to take the child away.

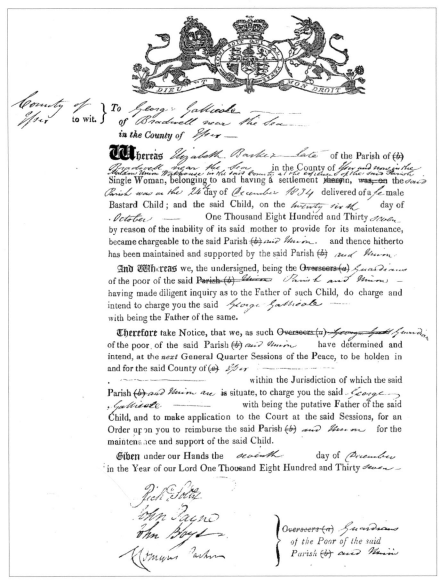

An official bastardy order issued by the parish, detailing monies required to be given by the father to the mother for the upkeep of his child. (*Essex Record Office*)

As records go there is no satisfactory outcome to this case. Was John Stebbing a man of position who could give the child a better home, or a scoundrel wishing to clear his name at all costs? Whichever, there is a twist to this tale. Sometime during the proceedings, Margery had confessed to a good friend of John Stebbing that she had not reported him as the father of her child, but that Mr Rust, the clerk, and her new master Robert Biggs of Felsted, had told her to say it was him.

Was Margery's indiscretion a perfect foil for a wider personal vendetta? If so, those concerned certainly gained by her disgrace. But not Margery; hers was to be a very public humiliation. It is interesting to note that the men who labelled Margery a 'lewd' woman were behaving in no less a lewd fashion by having her flogged half-naked through the streets.

ALSE MATHEWE

Geoffrey, the bastard son of Sarah Crispe a young and impudent whore of this parish!

(Fobbing Baptismal Register, 1758)

Duplicity was rife in cases of bastardy. In September 1588, Alse Mathewe also found herself before Justice of the Peace Israel Amyce, but unlike Margery Hawles, Alse escaped a flogging when she found support from an unlikely quarter.

Dismissed from service for being pregnant, Alse was forced to roam the countryside until she found herself in the parish of Belchamp St Paul where she managed to beg for relief for three days, before her situation came to the attention of the constables. Noting her condition, Mr Fryer and Mr Wilson demanded to know who she was and where she had come from. Alse explained her situation, citing her former master Robert Gosnold as the father of her child. That was in the morning. In the afternoon of the same day, in 'great sorrow', she confessed the real father to be Davy Cox, a fellow servant with whom she thought she had fallen in love. The constables then demanded to know if Davy Cox could support her and the child; Alse replied that he was sixteen, destitute of friends, like herself, and very, very poor.

Whether it was out of genuine concern or the desire to prevent maintenance for Alse and her child falling on the parish, Mr Fryer and Mr Wilson then 'earnestly persuaded' Alse not to charge such a beggarly fellow, but instead name a man that could well afford to keep her.

When Alse asked whom she should name, the constables strongly suggested she stand 'steadfast by her lie' and accuse her master. If she did this, they assured her, money and justice would certainly come her way. If she did not, they would whip her out of the parish.

Although Alse did not have much of a choice, she did not have to make up her mind immediately. A month later, Mr Fryer was still promising that he could procure money for her upkeep. Apparently he had done this sort of thing before. In persuading another poor wench to wrongly accuse her neighbour, Mr Fryer, then requesting money on her behalf, had seen the unfortunate man give it willingly rather than have his reputation brought into question. Such was the fear of some local constables that the maintenance of a base-born child should fall on their parish.

In the Easter session rolls of 1629, a young unmarried woman, Thomasin Mathewes, was staying with her mother in Pagglesham and 'fell into labour'. Her labour continued for three days during which time she was subjected to the 'fearful threatenings' of Richard Gale, one of the 'collectors', who demanded she leave the parish immediately or he would set fire to the roof over her head! It appears that others of the parish were in agreement, as she was 'constrained though with great danger to her life at the instant of her delivery and removed to a barn in Great Stambridge where she gave birth'. She returned the same day with her child to her mother's, where despite the incident she was lawfully settled. The resulting bastardy order decreed that the child be 'kept by her care and by her pains and industry'.

Sometimes the stigma and trouble of a birth out of wedlock were simply too much to bear. For Martha Coombs, the pressures of living in her time were insurmountable. In an inquisition dated Christmas Eve 1656 at the Assize court in Chelmsford, Martha was accused of giving birth on 18 December to a female bastard child whom, it was said, she strangled. Though she pleaded not guilty, she was ordered to be hanged.

Severity towards unwed mothers is also harshly expressed on a page in the Fobbing Baptismal Register, dated July 26 1758: 'Geoffrey, the bastard son of Sarah Crispe a young and impudent whore of this parish!'

5

WOMEN OF REASON
AND REFORM

ELIZABETH FRY, PRISON REFORMER (1780–1845)

I have lately been twice to Newgate to see after the poor prisoners who had poor little infants without clothing, or with very little and think if you saw how small a piece of bread they are each allowed a day you would be very sorry.

(Elizabeth Fry, in a letter to three of her children, 1813)

For those incarcerated in the semi-darkness and squalor of London's infamous prison, the appearance of the lady who had come to survey them must have aroused animosity, curiosity and suspicion. For Elizabeth Fry, that first visit to Newgate was a revelation, albeit a harsh one. Nothing had prepared her for the smell of unwashed bodies, urine and excrement, alcohol and rancid food, sweat, blood and vomit. Nor for the hundreds of drunken, rag-clad women crowded into four rooms built for half their number, the innocent awaiting trial side by side with hardened prostitutes and thieves, children with nowhere else to go, and babies born in prison fastened to empty breasts. She even witnessed one dead infant being stripped of his meager clothing so that it could be given to another child. Despite not being able to forget what she had seen in Newgate, it would be a further four years before she could return.

Elizabeth was born on 21 May 1780, the third child of Catherine and Joseph Gurney, a wealthy Quaker merchant. Throughout her childhood and adolescence, Elizabeth was a reluctant Quaker, wearing fashionable clothes and struggling with her faith. But her attitude changed in 1798 when (while wearing purple boots with scarlet laces!) she heard William Savery, an American Quaker, speak in a meeting and felt herself drawn towards the 'plain' Quakerism she had always resisted. When a friend prophesied that she would, in the future, become 'a light to the blind, speech to the dumb and feet to the lame', Elizabeth finally decided to fully embrace her faith. Well educated (her mother Catherine had always advocated that education should be for both boys and girls), Elizabeth began taking an interest in the poor and the sick, and she started a Sunday school in the laundry room of the family home in Earlham. The children – many already working in factories – to whom she told Bible stories and taught to read and write, were called 'Betsy's imps' by her sisters.

In the summer of 1799, Elizabeth received a proposal of marriage from Joseph Fry, the son of another wealthy Quaker family who were tea and spice merchants and her father's shared banking interests. Initially, Elizabeth refused Joseph, finding the shy young man too dull. But the solid and dependable Joseph was persistent and eventually, once she realised she did indeed love him dearly, they were married on 18 August 1800.

At first, Elizabeth and Joseph lived in St Mildred's Court, London, with Joseph's parents and surrounded by relatives. Katherine, the newlyweds' daughter, arrived in August 1801; she was the first of eight children born to Elizabeth between 1801 and 1812, a figure that would rise to eleven over twenty years. Constant child bearing and the demands of a large family ruined the health of many women in those days, so Elizabeth was fortunate to have the help of many servants and family members. Like many women, at times she felt her life was being taken over by motherhood. She loved her children and missed them when away, but wrote in her diary that she feared she might become 'the careworn and oppressed mother', especially as her last child Daniel (called Harry) was born in 1822, the same day as her first grandchild.

By 1811, the family had moved to Plashet in Essex where they would stay until 1831. In March 1811, a month after the birth of her seventh child, Elizabeth was recorded as an approved Quaker minister. She had also opened a much-needed girls' school opposite the gates of Plashet House. Despite her work with the poor and sick and being busily engaged in the duties of wife and mother, by 1812 she had begun to feel her life was 'slipping away to little purpose'. It was at this point that a family friend, appalled at what he himself had seen at Newgate prison, had turned to Elizabeth for ways of providing some form of comfort to the inmates. In 1813, Elizabeth made the visit that was to eventually reform prison conditions up and down the country.

It was Christmas 1816 before she could make a second visit. She had given birth to two more children by then and there had been trouble with the family business. The death of Elizabeth's daughter Betsy, aged only four years old, had for a while left her drained and melancholic. When the turnkey opened the door to the Female Quarter at Newgate, she saw that nothing had changed. If anything, conditions were even worse than before. Many of the ordinary women prisoners were drunk, due to the availability of cheap gin, and some were clearly deranged. Discipline was nonexistent, bullies ran the wards, fights and curses erupted freely. Many of the women strutted around in men's clothes. Even the tough male prisoners, who mingled with the women during the day, were appalled at their behaviour.

The women in the Female Quarter were typically waiting for transfer to the prison ships that would take them to the Colonies. Women of all ages were brought from county prisons in the south of England to await transportation, and some were kept there for weeks or months until a ship was available. They were kept in leg irons if they could not afford to pay the Keeper of Newgate for 'easement', and the turnkeys made a good living out of 'shaking down' (charging) prisoners for the most basic of necessities. Prisoners had to pay to be released when their sentence was over; the same charge was applied even if a prisoner had died. If no money was forthcoming the rotting corpse remained imprisoned. A few pennies or sexual favours could pay for meagre amenities or drink to dull the torment of imprisonment, but soap and water were scarce. Lice swarmed in clothes and hair. The daily ration of food was one small loaf of bread per person. There were no medicines. Sick women were dumped on dirty straw without so much as a bed. Death by 'prison fever' (typhus) was common.

Elizabeth documented her work at Newgate in journals, which she kept all her life. In 1817 she wrote:

I have just returned from a most melancholy visit to Newgate, where I have been at the request of Elizabeth Fricker (condemned for robbery), previous to her execution tomorrow morning, at eight o'clock. I found her much hurried, distressed and tormented in mind. Her hands cold and covered with something like the perspiration preceding death and in a universal tremor. The woman with her said she had been so outrageous before our going that they thought a man must be sent for to manage her. However, after a serious time with her, her troubled soul became calmed ... Besides this poor woman there are also six men to be hanged, one of whom has a wife near her confinement, also condemned and six young children. Since the awful report came down he has become quite mad, from horror of mind. A strait waistcoat could not keep him within bounds: he had just bitten the turnkey.

Elizabeth also appealed for the lives of women sentenced to be hanged. If her pleas were unsuccessful, she accompanied them to the scaffold and comforted them in their last moments.

I have lately been occupied in forming a school in Newgate for the children of the poor prisoners as well as the young criminals, which has brought much peace and satisfaction with it; but my mind has also been deeply affected in attending a poor woman who was executed this morning. I visited her twice; this event has brought me into much feeling by some distressingly nervous sensations in the night, so that this has been a time of deep humiliation to me, this witnessing the effect of the consequences of sin. The poor creature murdered her baby; and how inexpressibly awful now to have her life taken away.

(24 February 1817)

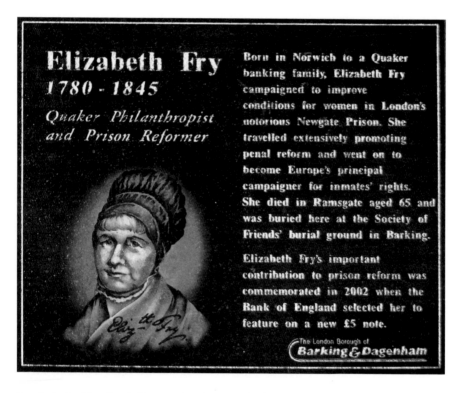

Elizabeth Fry

1780 - 1845

Quaker Philanthropist and Prison Reformer

Born in Norwich to a Quaker banking family, Elizabeth Fry campaigned to improve conditions for women in London's notorious Newgate Prison. She travelled extensively promoting penal reform and went on to become Europe's principal campaigner for inmates' rights. She died in Ramsgate aged 65 and was buried here at the Society of Friends' burial ground in Barking.

Elizabeth Fry's important contribution to prison reform was commemorated in 2002 when the Bank of England selected her to feature on a new £5 note.

The London Borough of
Barking & Dagenham

In 1876, the *New York Times* printed an article describing the conditions that Elizabeth Fry had found on her second visit to Newgate in 1817. Two cells which contained the female prisoners were barely 190 square yards and housed 300 women with their numerous children. Here they lived, slept, and washed, begging from visiting strangers in order to pay for the spirits that were available from a tap in the prison. At the gates outside the prison, Elizabeth had informed the guard that she was there not to judge but to offer comfort to the wretched women within. The turnkey had shaken his head. 'You should not go in alone, ma'am. They'll tear off your things and scratch and claw you. And first of all they'll snatch your watch.'

Elizabeth's school was set up as part of her 'Association for the improvement of the female prisoners in Newgate', which also arranged for a woman to be appointed as matron to supervise the prisoners. The Association also provided materials so that the prisoners could sew, knit and make goods for sale in order to buy food, clothing and fresh straw for bedding. Members of the Association took it in turns to visit the prison each day and to read from the Bible, believing that hearing the Bible had the power to reform people. When they applied to the Corporation of London for funding for the school, the Lord Mayor of London came to hear Elizabeth reading the Bible to the prisoners and he was so impressed by the women's good behaviour, he agreed to pay part of the matron's wages.

On one occasion when Elizabeth visited Newgate in 1818, she found some of the prisoners were about to riot because the next day they would be taken in 'irons' on open wagons to the ships that would carry them to Australia. Elizabeth Fry arranged for them to be taken in closed carriages to protect them from the stones and jeers of the crowds, and promised to go with them to the docks. From then on, when a group of women were sentenced to transportation, Elizabeth, in the weeks leading up to departure, made sure that ladies of the Association visited daily and provided each prisoner with a 'useful bag' of things the prisoners would need. They made patchwork quilts on the voyage, which were sold on arrival to provide some income. During the next twenty years, Elizabeth visited 106 convict ships that set sail for the Australias.

Elizabeth Fry had become something of a celebrity in Britain, but despite her obvious commitment to her family and her children, she was criticised for neglecting them in favour of what was considered by many to be a man's role. She herself confided to her journals that 'my mind is much taken up with Newgate' and that she had concerns over the waywardness of some of her children.

> Another sorrow just now is learning that I have not one child much under the influence of grace, or that appear to be bending to the cross. It is difficult to know how in all things to conduct myself toward them, to be neither too strict or too much the reverse.

Another entry showed her to be

> at home with my children, a great and very precious charge; at times they appear too much for me, at others I greatly enjoy them; I desire that the anxiety for their welfare, and to have them in order, should not prevent my enjoying thankfully, the blessings of being surrounded by so sweet a flock.

Much of the criticism was from Quakers who thought her involvement with the prison women was undignified.

In 1818, she was asked to give evidence to a House of Commons Committee on London prisons, the first woman to do so. This was the start of a period of Elizabeth Fry's life when she had extraordinary influence for a woman of her day. She described in detail the lives of the prisoners and gave a good account of her reforms, stressing her belief in the importance of useful employment.

> Our rules have certainly been occasionally broken, but very seldom; order has been generally observed; I think I may say we have full power amongst them, for one of them said it was more terrible to be brought up before me than before the judge, though we use nothing but kindness; I have never punished a woman during the whole time, or even proposed a punishment to them; and yet I think it is impossible, in a well-regulated house, to have rules more strictly attended to than they are, as far as I order them, or our friends in general. With regard to our work, they have made nearly twenty thousand articles of wearing apparel, the generality of which is supplied by the slop shops, which pays very little. Excepting three out of this number of articles that were missing, which we really do not think owing to the women, we have never lost a single thing. They knit from about 60 to a 100 pair of stockings and socks, every month; they spin a little. The earnings of their work, we think, average about eighteen-pence per week for each person. This is generally spent in assisting them to live, and helping to clothe them. For this purpose they subscribe, out of their small earnings of work, about four pounds a month, and we subscribe about eight, which keeps them covered and decent.

As well as her work with prisoners, Elizabeth Fry set up District Visiting Societies to work with the poor, libraries for coastguards, and a training school for nurses. When a small boy was found frozen to death near her home, she set up another Ladies Committee to offer hot soup and a bed to homeless women and children.

News of what she had achieved at Newgate led to the setting up of Ladies Committees in other towns in Britain and in Europe. Even Queen Victoria gave Elizabeth Fry a royal 'audience' and made a donation of £50 to her causes. But Elizabeth's life was not without personal difficulties. All her life she had suffered attacks of nervous depression and often found it necessary to ingest stimulants and sedatives in order to carry on her tasks. In 1828, when Joseph Fry went bankrupt, Elizabeth was humiliated. She found it hard to accept that God had allowed this to happen when she had obeyed his calling without question.

Elizabeth travelled extensively in western Europe in the 1830s, but continued to take on many other causes, such as the homeless of London, improvements for patients in mental asylums, and reforms of workhouses and hospitals. In 1840, in an effort to improve nursing standards, she started a training school in Guy's Hospital. The nurses that attended this school were expected to attend to both the physical and spiritual needs of their patients. Someone influenced by this pioneering method was Florence Nightingale; during the Crimean War, a number of 'Fry nurses' worked with Nightingale, caring for sick and wounded soldiers.

Elizabeth herself became ill in 1845 and eventually died on 12 October that same year. Quakers do not hold funeral services, but nevertheless around a thousand people maintained a respectful silence as she was buried in the Society of Friends graveyard at Barking.

On 24 October 1845, the *Chelmsford Chronicle* reported that the address given at the service for Elizabeth Fry was over two hours long and well received: 'all there were anxious to pay tribute to one whose life was marked by every virtue'.

Elizabeth's life today is not hard to forget. In 2002 she was awarded the ultimate honour of being depicted on the reverse of £5 notes issued by the Bank of England.

ANNE KNIGHT, ANTI-SLAVERY AND WOMEN'S RIGHTS CAMPAIGNER (1786–1862)

Her appearance was very singular, middle height and rather short when I knew her, with massive features and a countenance expressive of power. Rich personal voice and manners, though plain were attractive and from long residence abroad slightly foreign. She dressed in black and as plain as a Quaker with a bonnet of the strictest conformity, flowing dress and shawl, a large outside bag, or pocket, of black silk hung at her side suspended from her waist-belt in which she kept a quantity of pages which were produced as required in conversation.

(A contemporary account in Family Records by Charlotte Sturge, 1882)

According to *Pigot's Trade Directory of Essex 1832-3*, Chelmsford was a county town 'of high respectability', abounding 'with wealthy and genteel families'. William Knight, a prosperous wholesale grocer, was one such resident. Settling here and marrying Priscilla Allen, the daughter of a radical non-conformist, he fathered eight children. One of his daughters, Anne, born in 1786, was to spend most of her life championing the major social reforms of her age.

As a young woman, Anne was strong-minded and free-spirited, her Quaker background setting her apart from the sheltered 'Jane Austin' existence of most middle class women of her time. Independent and controversial, with an 'eccentricity of character' inherited from her mother, Anne was soon fuelled by a desire for social reform. Though she pursued this all her life, she never quite achieved the political greatness she deserved. Not until the 1970s, when women became more conscious of their legal rights or continued lack of them, was she hailed as the formidable grass roots social campaigner she had always been.

Anne spent her childhood and most of her adult life at the family home in Chelmsford. She never married. Maybe it was her father's 'long suffering' relationship with her mother that led to her to choose the state of 'single blessedness' that she referred to in her letters, or perhaps it was her support of the Temperence Movement. The 'Volsted Act' or 'the manufacture, sale, or transportation of intoxicating liquors', better known as Prohibition, which made drink illegal in America in 1919, was yet to come. When Anne was involved in this transatlantic movement it concerned itself more with domestic violence and the financial hardship associated with addiction to alcohol.

Anne was appalled at the rapid spread of this social scourge and the complacency of the law. The legal system was based upon the idea that

Drink and drunkenness were the main causes of domestic violence in the nineteenth century. Unregulated drinking hours and cheap spirits were to blame. Not until the First World War were drinking hours reduced.

women married, had children, and were looked after by their husbands, but when this ideal failed, legislation did not exist to protect them. Men had the right to control their wives by force, to beat and imprison them in the matrimonial home if necessary. As the law stood, whenever it was called to intervene in domestic disputes it was only to restrain violence, not prevent it. Anne, as early as the 1830s, was a passionate advocate for votes for women, but it would be her fight for the abolition of slavery that eventually propelled her into becoming an early champion of women's suffrage.

Through family contact with Quakers nationwide and the acquaintance of local Abolitionist Joseph Marriage, a member of Chelmsford's increasingly successful milling and farming family, Anne began raising her voice at anti-slavery rallies and corresponding with other women campaigners both in Europe and in America. For Anne, slavery was a social issue, not just a moral one. In 1831, she founded the Chelmsford branch of the national Anti-Slavery Society, one of seventy-three such women's organisations set up around the country.

Her support for the 'cause' was fervent; she canvassed from door to door, arranged public meetings, printed leaflets, distributed literature, and travelled frequently to London. Here she met and worked with national leaders, among them Thomas Clarkson.

It was Clarkson, who along with Granville Sharp had set up the original Society for the Abolition of the Slave Trade in 1787. For two years he had travelled the length and breadth of Britain, gathering the evidence needed to support the abolitionist argument, leaving no stone unturned. He covered 35,000 miles and collected equipment used on the slave-ships such as iron handcuffs, leg-shackles, thumbscrews, instruments for forcing open slaves' jaws, and branding irons. Polite society was duly shocked. They were also embarrassed to learn that Britain was the biggest transporter of slaves across the Atlantic and that the 'middle passage' or nine-week voyage from England to American regularly claimed the lives of half the slaves on board. They were also told that a half cargo of slaves posed a serious financial loss to the trader and so the remaining slaves were then chained together and thrown overboard, all for a handsome compensation.

Clarkson had also added weight to his argument by interviewing 20,000 sailors in ports such a Bristol and Liverpool, discovering the slave trade was not a 'business seamen joined from preference.' He cited the British government as treating 'the sons of Neptune' as little more than slaves themselves, calling for the cessation of 'crimping' – the practice of merchants paying tavern keepers to entice the innocent into 'their infamous dens where every allurement and artifice is held out', and the practice of then 'recruiting men through the press'.

The Abolition of the Slave Trade Act was eventually passed in 1807, but it was not until 1833 that Parliament passed the Slavery Abolition Act that gave all slaves in the British Empire their freedom.

Anne and other early women activists now campaigned for the end to colonial slavery on the back of what had become an overwhelmingly male success. But she found discrimination in many quarters. Early leaders of the Society such as William Wilberforce were unhappy at women meddling in the Society. He opposed the women's call for total abolition, preferring first to bring about the cessation of the trade. In 1826, he had written a letter expressing his doubts about women such as Anne Knight. 'For ladies to meet, to publish, to go from house to house stirring up petitions – these appear to me proceedings unsuited to the female character as delineated in Scripture.' Concerned there was not sufficient infrastructure or education in place to rehabilitate slaves, Wilberforce feared immediate abolition would end in chaos, and thus be counterproductive to the cause.

Anne and her female colleagues found themselves marginalised, but not by all. When George Thompson, the famous abolitionist orator, regretfully declined Anne's request for him to address an important women's lobby, he praised her contributions to the Society and was generous towards the female anti-slavery associations. 'Where they exist,' he said, 'they are everything. In a word, they form the cement of the whole anti-slavery building – without your aid we never should have been united.' Not one to be deterred, Anne went on to undertake a speaking tour of France herself. As for George Thompson, it was probably he who recommended that one of the newly founded villages for freed men in Jamaica be named Knightsville in Anne's honour.

Anne continued to campaign alongside other female abolitionists such as Elizabeth Heyrick, Jane Smeal, Anne Taylor Gilbert, and Elizabeth Pease, but when women were refused admission to the World Anti-Slavery Convention held in London in 1841, Anne's thoughts again returned to the pressing need for women's rights. Contacts she had made over the years, both male and female, while supporting the anti-slavery movement, now helped her to champion the feminist cause with equal enthusiasm. Her letters were read on both sides of the Atlantic and she brought statements on sex equality to the public attention by writing them on brightly coloured labels, which she then stuck on to the envelopes of her letters. Pointing out that 'the young women of the Gauls had the right to make the laws', that 'Anglo-Saxon women participated in their legislature', and in one of the strongest North American tribes 'women of the Hurons, made up a great council and the elders followed their advice ... while we struggle for liberty!' These statements were aimed at shaming men into remembering that women had not always been so undervalued.

Courageously, Anne demanded emancipation and female enfranchisement. She wanted an end to the laws that saw women pass seamlessly from father to husband, their wealth and earnings, even their children, never their own. She called for equal rights for a woman to divorce a husband for adultery, and an end to the legislation that allowed men to 'chastise' their wives with 'any reasonable instrument'. But Anne's outrage alone could not bring about change. Women would have to wait until 1882 and the Married Property Act to see any real change in their rights.

In 1846, fearing the Reform movement in Britain had become too conservative, Anne left Chelmsford and her Essex roots for France. Though now over fifty years old, she had lost none of her energy; in befriending other women activists, she continued to push women's issues forward, campaigning for equal access to education, employment, and a woman's right to sit in parliament. In 1847, in what is believed to be the first ever leaflet on women's suffrage, she wrote: 'Never will the nations of the earth be well governed until both sexes, as well as all parties, are fully represented, and have an influence, a voice, and a hand in the enactment and administration of the laws.' Three years later, on 9 February 1850, the *Brighton Herald* published a letter in which she stated: 'It is justice that we demand for all who bear their share in the burdens of the State, and who does not pay taxes in this miserably tax-ground country? Is she exempt whose part it is to work 18 hours out of 24, to sleep little, and to be too much worn with labour to think?'

Anne died on 4 November 1862, spending the last few years of her life in the small village of Waldersbach, south-west of Strasbourg. Had it not been for the recent discovery of her letters, the life and work of this Essex girl would have stayed largely unknown. Today, Chelmsford is recognising her contribution to social reform by immortalising her name in bricks and mortar. Anne Knight House is the newest accommodation house for students on the University of Essex's recently extended campus. The Colchester Quaker Housing Association also has named their new hostel in Chelmsford after the town's most famous daughter.

Let us not be urged to prick our fingers to the bone in sewing circles for Vanity Fair, Peace Bazaars, where health and mind equally suffer in the sedentary stitch, stitch, stitch, ever toiling while our poor brother is groping his way in darkness without the good sense and clear discernment of his sister at his side.

(Anne Knight)

6

WOMEN OF COURAGE AND ENDEAVOUR

HANNAH LAKE, NEW WORLD SETTLER
(1621–c.1675)

You cannot get a much smaller village in Essex today than North Benfleet. With its hilltop church and linear settlement strung out along a single lane, it is hard to believe anything here could come to public attention, let alone be involved in global events. But from this tiny place on the edges of the South Essex marshes, Hannah Lake set out on a daunting three-month sea voyage to the other side of the known world. A traceable ancestor of the two Bush presidents of the United States, she would become a founding 'mother' of America.

Nowhere in England was the religious upheaval and civil unrest of the early seventeenth century more evident than in Essex. The stability and statesmanship of the Tudor dynasty had been replaced with confrontation and persecution by a dour and pedantic James I, and the Gunpowder Plot of 1605 was an early indication of the low esteem in which some Englishmen held their new Scottish king. James' son Charles I fared no better in the hearts and minds of the British people. As a Protestant with a French wife, his tolerance of her Catholic faith made those in power suspicious of a papist plot to seize the government. Feelings against Rome rose dangerously high. Religious persecution, especially in Essex, took the form of fines, imprisonment in Colchester Castle, and land seizures from recusants. It meant death for priests who administered the sacraments in secret chapels or open air meetings. In the wake of such harsh penalties, the years preceding the Civil War saw upward of 30,000 people leave England for new lives in the Americas.

The parish registers of North Benfleet's All Saints' church record Hannah Lake's birth/baptism on 3 July 1621. The Lake family were yeoman farmers, and had been for many generations. Hannah's grandfather, the

Sometime between 1616 and 1621, Hannah's father, John Lake, inherited Fanton Hall Farm. Hannah's baptism/birth is recorded in North Benfleet church on the other side of the A127 arterial road which effectively cut the parish in half when it was constructed in 1928.

respected John Lake, served as juror for Barstable Hundred in the year of the Armada, 1588, while his son, also John Lake, was described in later documents as 'gent'. He owned lands in Nevendon and Basildon, brought to the family by his mother Elizabeth Sandel, and in Wickford and Rawreth, the dowry of his wife Margaret, whom he married when she was eighteen and he twenty-six.

Today, All Saints' church and its manor of Fann or Fanton Hall lie on separate sides of the A127 London to Southend arterial road; this road's construction in 1928 effectively split the parish in half. Sometime between 1616 and 1621, Hannah's father, the eldest of his brothers, inherited Fanton Hall from his father. Here, on the profitable manor farm (it still consisted of 303 acres as late as 1926), Hannah, one of Margaret and John's eight children, grew up.

John was the first of the Lake children to be born at Wickford. Margaret must have fallen pregnant almost as soon as John was born as Thomas, her second son, was baptised in January of the year 1617/18. A third son, Richard, was baptised on 21 May 1620, but he died within hours. Hannah, Margaret's first daughter, was born in 1621 and baptised at All Saints' in North Benfleet, the church connected to Fanton Hall, the new Lake family residence. Another girl followed only to be buried within days of her birth in August 1623. Martha, the sister that accompanied Hannah and her mother to America, was baptised in July of 1624. Samuel and Elizabeth were both born within the next eighteen months, but did not survive infancy. Perhaps miscarriages account for the five-year gap before another son was born; this boy also died within a month. Of Margaret's eight children in thirteen years, only four survived to adulthood. This was not unusual in the seventeenth century. Had she not left for America, she might have gone on to bear many more children (she was still only in her early thirties at the time her migration).

Hannah's Essex was one of both wealth and poverty. As landowners, the Lakes could rely on a good income from rents and leases. This would have made Hannah's situation and that of her family at least comfortable. So what had induced Hannah's mother, Margaret, to take her two daughters to the other side of the known world and expose them to the dangers and uncertainties of the colonies? What had made her so brave?

It's most likely that Margaret looked to the colonies as a sanctuary for her beliefs. Margaret and her two daughters, Hannah and Martha, made their journey to America around 1635 as part of what today is known as the 'Great Migration'. This wholesale exodus had begun in 1630 when John Winthrop Sr and a small fleet of Puritan settlers founded the Massachusetts Bay Colony, paving the way for many more to follow. Courage would have been needed to settle in an unknown wilderness following a perilous Atlantic crossing; Margaret's conviction would have been bolstered by the fact that she was travelling to the New World with her sister Elizabeth Reade, who had invited her to join her and her new husband John Winthrop Jr in their migration.

Elizabeth's marriage to John Winthrop Jr was to connect the Lakes and Reades of North Benfleet to a most prestigious family. It was John's second marriage; his first to Martha Fones of Great Stambridge had ended with her death and the death of their baby daughter in childbirth. His marriage to the young Elizabeth Reade had taken place on a trip to England on family business. Margaret and her daughters were to live with the Winthrops until Hannah and Martha married, Margaret herself residing under her brother-in-law's protection until he became Governor of Connecticut. For John Winthrop Jr, this trip to the New World was a return journey. For Elizabeth, Margaret, Hannah and Martha, it would be their first step into the unknown.

Equally, though controversial for the time, Margaret could well have viewed the Americas as her refuge from an unhappy marriage. Some records have her as a widow at the time of her departure from England, yet correspondence she received almost twenty years later in around 1654 informed her that 'John Lake is alive and lusty' and again in 1657 that 'John Lake still lives'.

In 1661/62, she wrote to family in London from her home in Massachusetts with regard to her husband's death and 'how he ended his dayes', inquiring of her cousin 'whether their was anything left mee or no'.

The circumstances surrounding Margaret's decision to leave England with her daughters leave some important questions unanswered. The information she received that 'John Lake is alive and lusty' could also have been news of her first-born son, also called John, whom she had not seen for almost twenty years. He was eighteen when she left and in line to inherit the Lake estates so did not accompany her. The truth was that at about this time he had been disinherited as heir to Fanton Hall and the family lands in Barstable Hundred for not finishing his education. If Margaret put her maternal instincts towards her first born son before her loyalty to her husband in this issue, the resulting marital conflict may have been the deciding factor in her decision to leave. It may have been that she left England with a heavy heart. Perhaps from that point on, 'widow' is how she saw herself. On a positive note, it would definitely have been a safer label under which to travel.

The new world in which Margaret and her daughters first found themselves was the tribal homeland of the Wampanoag Indians. Boston, fast becoming a sizable settlement, had wharves able to support ship building and a good harbour, often with up to eight vessels at anchor. Building material was in good supply (unlike Europe where wood was now costly) and, with saw mills located on the plentiful streams and rivers, even the poorest family could enjoy a two storey house with a hall, parlour, and kitchen, as well as 'doors high enough to enter without stooping'. Adjacent colonies of Ipswich and Braintree were no more than thirty miles away; although travel on land was hazardous, usually following Indian trackways which dipped in and out of the wilderness, journeys could be made quite safely by boat along the coast.

By 1637, the Massachusetts Bay Colony had conquered the Indian tribes of eastern Connecticut and, needing to bring this new land under their control (as well as wishing to keep the Dutch at bay), they gave John Winthrop Jr land belonging to the Pequot Indians to set up a new colony. Eight years later, in 1645, when Winthrop visited this land to finalise his plans for the settlement, Margaret Reade accompanied him. Ten years after leaving Essex, she was the first European woman to set foot freely in what would later become known as New London.

For women in New England there was a great pressure to marry, and it wasn't unusual for girls to find a husband and begin to produce children before they reached twenty. Hannah was twenty-two when she married John Gallop in 1643 in her uncle John Winthrop's house in Boston. It was a simple civil ceremony involving no more than the holding of hands before a magistrate and then being announced as man and wife. Evidently, the people of New England saw nothing in their Christian teachings that made it necessary for a wedding to be presided over by a priest.

Despite the pressures to marry, opportunities for young men and women to socialise were almost nil. It was, in fact, prohibited on Sundays. Courtship required the permission of the woman's father and if this was not observed, the suitor could be legally penalised. Strangely though, 'bundling' was permitted. If a courtship was agreed, then, due to a general lack of privacy in most New England houses, the couple were allowed to share the same bed, but fully clothed, sometimes with the male sewn into a large sack, and with a log divider between them on top of the blankets. Such a practice would then allow the couple to converse and exchange endearments, but not allow them to indulge in indiscretions.

Whether Hannah experienced 'bundling' is not known, but in marrying John Gallop she became part of a frontier family whose contribution to the early colonisation of Boston was invaluable. As part of Winthrop's original fleet, her father-in-law had arrived aboard the *Mary & John* and had soon become the owner of a house and a wharf at what became known as Gallop's Point.

John's mother, Christobel Bruschett, had been reluctant at first to leave her home in England, possibly due to the young age of her children. Fearing his wife would not join him, John Gallop Sr prepared to return to England. However, Gallop's navigational skills were proving vital to the successful development of trade between the Massachusetts Bay Colony, Connecticut and Rhode Island, and John Winthrop Sr was very reluctant to see him go. He wrote to Revd John White in England, asking if he would persuade Gallop's wife to join her husband in New England: 'I have much difficultye to keep John Gallop here by reason of his wife will not come', adding, perhaps not fully appreciating a mother's protective instincts, 'I marvayle at the woman's weaknesse that she will live miserably with her children there, when she might live comfortably here with her husband.' Christobel landed in Boston harbour aboard the *Griffin* on 4 September 1633.

Hannah's husband, John Gallop, had taken wholeheartedly to frontier life. Even today the citizens of the New England states consider him to have been a very brave man. A mariner and trader like his father, he was also an Indian interpreter and even at the tender age of sixteen he was involved, with his father, in incidents that led to the ultimate conflict of the English with the Mohegan, Narragansett, and Pequot Indian tribes.

Once married, Hannah and John moved south from Boston and settled in Taunton, part of the Plymouth colony. Here the first of the couple's ten children, Hannah, was born on 14 September 1644, followed by a son, John, a year later. Both children were baptised in Boston, possibly because it was far safer for Hannah to return to her mother and relative civilization for the births. In 1651, John Gallop Sr died and Hannah's husband John became heir to a handsome land-grant awarded by the Massachusetts Bay Colony to veterans of the Pequot Wars. This land was part of John Winthrop's plantation of New London. Although it was already a viable settlement of sixty families when they got there, they were nevertheless allotted a generous eight acre plot within the town, a full two acres more than any others had received. As Indian treaties were made and land was cleared in river valleys and along the coasts of southern Connecticut, more land was allotted to the New London families who could choose to relocate or cultivate these farmsteads from the original settlement.

As wife to John Winthrop Jr, the governor of New London, Elizabeth Reede, Hannah's aunt, found herself mistress of a considerable amount of land. Within the Pequot plantation, she and her husband owned 13,000 acres. Within the village they had command of most of the river front, upon which John Winthrop sited his water powered gristmill, as well as 700 acres on the other side of the river. His largest tract of land was a stretch along the coast of Long Island, which was three miles deep going inland, opposite Fishers Island which he already owned.

In 1654, John, Hannah, and their three children (Esther had been born in 1653) settled on 300 acres of land given to them on the east bank of the Mystic River, preferring to make it their main dwelling place as it offered John a protected anchorage for his seafaring activities as well as land good for farming.

Contrary to this sounding like an idyll, frontier life was hard; Hannah would have had to be physically strong to survive childbearing and mentally strong to cope with the isolation, uncertainty, and the danger of her new surroundings.

The family unit was a crucial part of colonial life. Children were the future work force and women were expected to produce them. If a woman died in childbirth it was usually only a matter of weeks before the husband took a new wife to help with the remaining children; neighbours often intermarried to form strong alliances. Anything or anyone that destabilised the family was treated harshly, and a husband's authority in marriage was absolute. Although allowed to be church members, women were not allowed to speak in church; and in an age of superstition and fear, if all else failed, the tale of Anne Hutchinson – who was brutally scalped and murdered by Indians – was often cited by some Puritans to keep women in their place. Her violent death, as they saw it, was God's will because she meddled in things that did not concern her.

Having said this, when their menfolk were away it was up to wives to manage the homestead and at times defend it. Hannah would have been left alone for long periods while her husband was leading supply wagons or on trading expeditions. Though south-eastern Connecticut had been largely cleared of Indian villages, winter hunters of the Mohican and Narragansett tribes still followed tribal tracks across newly settled land and fished off the coast in summer.

Unlike in England, wolves were a very real danger. Whereas the largely nomadic Indians had co-existed with them for thousands of years, the settlers' economies depended on livestock; wolves were drawn to farmsteads for easy pickings, often harrying, and occasionally decimating, the animals. Hannah, as well as the other women, would have to have had extraordinary courage and faith in God's will to make her family prosper.

And prosper they did. Hannah's second son Benadam was born in 1655, and she went on to produce six more children: four girls and two boys. John rose to prominence representing their settlement of Stonington

Hannah's tomb in Whitehall cemetery, Mystic, Connecticut. She died a respected and wealthy woman aged fifty-four. A founding mother of the United States, Hannah is an ancestor of the two Bush presidents. (*Midge Frazel*)

Connecticut as its Deputy or 'selectman' in the years 1664 and 1667, and again in 1670/71. The couple was also awarded several more land grants during this time, bringing their land holdings into many hundreds of acres in consequence of John's own part in the Pequot Wars when he was younger.

It was not to be the only Indian war in which John Gallop fought. When, in 1675–76, a series of raids and skirmishes known as King Philip's War raged through the towns and villages of New England, Hannah's husband, despite being sixty years old, took command of the First Company of the Connecticut Regiment. One of six captains, he served in the Great Swamp Fight of 19 December 1676, but fell with his comrades while storming the Narragansett Fortress and was buried at nearby Wickford in a mass grave near the battlefield.

Hannah's sons, John and William, had also fought in King Phillip's War, continuing a tradition that would see her grandsons, great-grandsons and great-great-grandsons fight in the War of Independence and the American Civil War. Hannah's daughters too inherited their mother's fortitude, helping to carve out the American nation as it is today.

When Hannah Lake first set foot in the fledgling town of Boston as a young girl of fifteen, she had left behind the marshes and islands of south-eastern Essex. Forty years later, aged fifty-four, Hannah Gallop died a respected and wealthy woman, whose descendents would eventually include Presidents George H.W. and George W. Bush.

CONVICT WOMEN TRANSPORTED TO AUSTRALIA, 1787–1850

To fall foul of the law in Georgian and early Victorian England was to find yourself condemned by a harsh and brutal penal system. Suddenly on the other side of the world through no desire of their own, many women from Essex were among the 160,000 men, women, and children transported overseas between 1787 and 1868.

For England's tired and overcrowded legal system, transportation had always been an opportunity as well as a solution. Despatching miscreants to America had rid this country of an undesirable criminal populace and secured stabilisation and growth in the colonies. But in the wake of the American Revolution, that avenue was no longer open. In 1775, with the industrial revolution bringing more people to the cities and the subsequent increase in crime, the Secretary of State in Britain, Thomas Townsend, decided to establish a Penal Colony in Australia, discovered by Captain James Cook fifteen years earlier in 1770.

Essex County Gaol Chelmsford	*List of Female Convicts under sentence of Transportation, unfit to be removed.*		
Name	When tried	Offence	Sentence
Mary Holloway	Adjourned Session 23rd Feby. 1836	Stealing shoes &c	7 years Transportation
Sarah Lavender	Michas Session 1836	Housebreaking	14 years Transportation
			Wm. C. Neale

A notice from Chelmsford Gaol listing that Mary Bellamy and Sarah Lavender (sentenced to seven and fourteen years respectively) were deemed unfit to be transported at that time. Then, as today, it seems a prisoner had to be fit enough to survive the deprivations ahead of him or her. (*Essex Record Office*)

The British Government hired nine ships and two naval vessels and supplied them with enough provisions to sustain the 759 convicts, 180 of them women, their Marine guards, and a few civil officers to the 'lands beyond the seas', until they became self-sufficient. This first fleet left England in May 1787 and reached Australia in January the following year. Though deaths on board had been relatively few, the fledgling settlement was beset with problems in attaining food and water supplies once on dry land. With the transported labour force more attuned to felony than farming, soon everyone from the convicts to the Captain was on rationed food.

Ships of the second fleet, *Guardian, Justinian, Lady Juliana, Surprize, Neptune* and *Scarborough*, reached the struggling settlement by 1790, the *Justinian* loaded entirely with supplies and the 401 ton transport ship *Lady Juliana* laden with over 200 women. In view of the fragility of the new settlement, these female convicts had been sent with the view of stabilising and increasing the population of the colony. Healthy, strong, and of childbearing age, twenty-five-year-old Sarah Manning and twenty-nine-year-old Catherine Wilmot were among them. Both had been tried for their crimes at the Essex Lent Assizes two years before in 1788. Catherine, already a mother of four, had had her appeal turned down despite being described as 'quiet and industrious'. On the *Neptune*, which carried convicts of both sexes, Martha Brown and Sarah Smith were being transported for seven years.

Conditions on the *Lady Juliana* were only marginally better than her sister ships in the fleet, though much improved from the deprivations of Newgate and the provincial goals the women had left behind. Fresh air and regular meals meant neglect was not a cause of death on board, and the lack of segregation between the sexes, or 'open ship' policy, meant infighting through sexual frustration was greatly reduced. As the charitable ladies of London had donated fifty 'suits of child linen' to be used should they be needed, seven children were duly born on the voyage. These, along with the eight children already accompanying their mothers and the pregnancies which continued once the women were ashore, soon gained the *Lady Juliana* the name 'The Floating Brothel'.

Convicts on the vessels that lay beside the *Lady Juliana* anchored in Sydney Cove fared less favourably. Collectively, this second fleet was in the hands of private contractors; a document dated 1790 describes the 'diabolical condition of the convicts' as they came ashore. 'A sight most outrageous to our eyes were the marks of leg irons upon the convicts, some so deep that one could nigh on see the bones'. Whether such mistreatment was experienced by Essex women Martha Brown and Sarah Smith on the *Neptune* is not documented.

A prison hulk, moored off Deptford, where prisoners would await transportation.

Cruel masters, harsh discipline, scurvy, dysentery and typhoid resulted in a huge loss of life for convicts during the rest of the eighteenth century. Transportation, however, had become a popular method of dealing with overcrowded gaols and overloaded, reeking prison hulks; women from all over Essex increasingly found themselves as human cargo. Susan Coot and Catherine Mooney were aboard the *Mary Ann* which set sail from England in 1791, followed a year later by the *Pitt*, named after the then prime minister, carrying Mary House and Hannah Jackson. Elizabeth Brooks and Susannah Garnett were on board the *Britannia*, which arrived in 1798, and Sarah Tillet, one of fifty-three women on board the *Speedy*, first sighted the shores of New South Wales in April 1800 after 143 days at sea.

A review of the system in 1801 reduced the dispatch of ships to no more than twice a year in order to avoid unnecessary deaths caused by dangerous winters. Independent surgeons responsible for convict welfare were also employed. Sarah Haslen and Lydia Norman, aboard the *Nile* in 1801, may well have benefited from these improvements. Perhaps too, Mary Cable, Charlotte King, Elizabeth Wicker and Mary Daniels, pardoned in 1809, on their passage from England on 2 January 1804 aboard the *Experiment*. Mary Gibson arrived in 1810 having sailed on the *Canada*.

Susan Gage, also known as Susan Noon, was one of a hundred females aboard the *Friends* which sailed on 21 January 1811. Her crime was theft and deception. Claiming to work for a Mrs Walker, a respected woman of the town, she had gone into the shop of a Thomas Pod of Colchester and asked to 'view some stockings'. Susan had left the shop with seventeen pairs on approval and, to alleviate suspicion, actually returned with them later to say her mistress would have them all. Mr Pod, after wrapping the items, charged the ten shilling fee to Mrs Walker's account as Susan Gage had requested. Of course, Mrs Walker had never seen the stockings and Susan, tried on 30 April 1810 at Colchester Quarter Sessions, was transported for 7 years.

In 1814, the *Broxbornbury* brought Martha Banford and Harriet Holmes to New South Wales. The *Northampton* arrived on 18 June 1815 carrying 110 women, one of them Sarah Lawson.

Over the next four years, Maria Peacock, Jane Hewson, Deborah Lawden, Caroline Kensey and Niomi Wright joined their fellow convicts, sailing from Essex on the *Morley, Mary* and *Harmony*. Naomi's sentence had been commuted from death by hanging to transportation after being charged with breaking into a house along with her brothers George and Thomas and her sister-in-law Mary. Having stolen clothing and money exceeding £50, both George and Thomas were sent to Tasmania while Mary was acquitted. Both Sophie Kelly and Maria Cook had been tried and sentenced in Essex, arriving in Van Diemen's Land – latterly Tasmania – on 16 May 1826. Sophia, convicted at the Essex Quarter Sessions, only got seven years, but Maria, having been tried at the Assizes, was transported for life.

Just as today, crime in past centuries made good copy. The London *Times*, as well as local newspapers, featured lists of transportees as well as transcripts of court proceedings. For us in the modern world, the sentences meted out far outstrip the seriousness of the offence, even if those accused are guilty. One such incident was reported on 11 August 1829 in *The Essex Herald* under the heading 'Sheep Stealing'.

John Passaway was convicted of stealing a ewe sheep, the property of Thomas Mills, of Theydon Bois, and Millicent Sawkins was convicted of receiving the same, knowing it to be stolen. It appeared the two prisoners lived together as man and wife, in a cottage near the prosecutor's field. On the 15th of March, an ewe sheep was stolen from its lamb, and suspicion falling on Passaway, the house was searched; under a board in the floor was found part of the neck and shoulder, and other pieces of the carcass of a sheep. In a cupboard a quantity of mutton fat was discovered, and upon the fire by which the prisoners were sitting, a pot containing a loin and shoulder was boiling. In the direction from the prisoner's house to Mills's field, the skin of a ewe sheep, bearing the marks of the prosecutor, was found, and the meat was compared with it. A portion of the cup of the head was left upon the skin, which corresponded exactly with the flesh. The Jury recommended Sawkins to mercy, but the Learned Judge shook his head, saying, he believed her to be a very bad woman. In passing sentence upon Passaway, he observed that he had before been convicted of poaching, with which crime he had commenced his life. This, his Lordship said, was the beginning of all crime; it led first to sheep stealing then to horse stealing, and frequently ended in murder. Although it was probable his life would be spared, he would not be allowed to spend any more of it in this country – Death recorded. Sawkins 14 years' transportation.

Three years later the details of another Chelmsford trial appeared in the *Times*. Dated 10 March 1832, it described the accused, Mary Bloomfield, as an 'innocent looking country girl'.

Only sixteen, Mary was accused of stealing a petticoat and some ribbon from her master's house in West Bergholt. First suspected of starting the fire which engulfed his property the previous July, Mary was arrested and taken to Colchester Gaol. As part of the procedure, her belongings had been searched for things which could have caused the fire. There were none, but they did find the petticoat and ribbon that had gone missing. Found guilty on the strength of this evidence, she was then tried for another offence as a key, which opened all the cupboards in her master's house, had also been discovered. Accused of stealing items of china and glass from her employer, she was indicted along with an elderly local man named Jeremiah Peachy, who was supposed to have received the items knowing they were stolen. On searching the man's house, the items were recovered but charges were dropped when Sarah Peachy, his daughter, admitted it had been Mary and herself who had committed the crime. Having turned King's evidence, Sarah was treated leniently and Jeremiah cleared of all charges. Mary, found guilty a second time, was sentenced to fourteen years transportation.

Few women, if any, returned to the country that had treated them so harshly. Many served out their sentences as domestic servants, or within 'Female Factories' run on the workhouse principle where the women worked for their keep. Marriage was encouraged and in the early days of the colonies women fresh from the ship would be sold off or lined up and 'chosen' by male settlers and male convicts alike. As the years went by, women were at liberty to remarry as long as their husbands were abroad and there had been seven years separation. Mary Fillingham of Colchester married Henry Holbrook when she was forty years old, having been transported on the *Persian* in 1827.

If populating a colony was what many English bureaucrats had in mind when they first transported women to the land across the sea, they would surely have been pleased with Niomi Wright, mentioned above. Having escaped a death sentence in England for housebreaking and theft, she had married Charles Armstrong, a former convict, in August 1828, a year into her lifelong exile. They went on to have no less than twelve children. At the time of her death, seventy-one grandchildren and fifty-five great grandchildren were still living.

MARY JOSCELYNE,
A VERY SPECIAL MIDWIFE

When the difficult delivery was successfully ended, a stranger entered the room wearing a patch over one eye and with an empty sleeve to his jacket.

There has never been an easier time for a woman to have a child than today. Women have control over their fertility and can choose how, where, and even when to give birth, but this 'right' took a long time to win. For centuries, women diced with death throughout their childbearing years. Death was an 'expected' tragedy and mothers preparing for 'lying-in' would also prepare for their own or their child's death as routine. In the Middle Ages, midwifery was rife with superstition leading to accusations of witchcraft. Later, women's lives were blighted with birthing stools, darkened rooms, and isolation. Forceps, though designed to aid difficult deliveries, were only available to noble women, and pain relief was unheard of until the Victorian era when Queen Victoria – a great advocate of laughing gas – demanded anaesthesia whenever she gave birth.

To have avoided the complications of childbirth was a blessing indeed. But for some there were other 'complications'. Bigotry surrounded the condition, and in a male-dominated society to have a child out of wedlock was reason enough to be incarcerated, outcast, disinherited, or forced to conduct the pregnancy in secret.

It has long been rumoured that Leigh-on-Sea was the birth place of a 'secret' child born to Emma Hamilton and Lord Horatio Nelson. It is a claim shared with many places along the Essex coast. In Leigh, however, two pieces of evidence point to the likelihood of this tale being more than just speculation: the first, a record of a particular baby's birth in the registers of St Mary's, Prittlewell, and secondly, a woman called Mary Joscelyne.

Emma Hamilton, a portrait by Romney. As a contemporary artist of the time, Romney painted Emma as various characters, this one being called 'Nature'. It is said she secretly gave birth to Nelson's child at Southchurch Lawn with Mary Joscelyn in attendance.

Lady Hamilton and Horatio Nelson already had one child together, a daughter born illegitimately on 29 October 1800. She was christened Horatia Nelson Thompson as the first step in an elaborate deception to mask the scandal. The child was put into the care of a Mrs Gibson and given the name of Thompson or Tomson to suggest she was the reputed daughter of a seaman. The scheme worked and the world believed Nelson and Emma to be her godparents. Only they then adopted the child as an orphan.

The spring of 1804 sparked rumours that Emma Hamilton was again expecting a child. A regular visitor to the Royal Terrace in Southend, she favoured this stretch of coast as a place to receive Nelson when his ship was anchored off the Nore. When her time came she retired to a house not far from the coast, her condition once more a secret for fear of scandal. But in the wake of a difficult birth, help was needed and Mary Joscelyne found herself conveyed to Southchurch Lawn in a curtained coach in the dead of night, at twice her usual fee, to assist at the labour of a 'gentlewoman in distress'.

Mary was a natural choice. Southchurch Lawn was the home of her mother and stepfather. Mary's own father had died in 1769 leaving his widow with two surviving children out of five, Mary and her brother James. Three years later, in 1772, Mary's mother Elizabeth married Christopher Parson, a wealthy farmer of 600 acres. He was also a barge owner and builder and lord of the Southchurch parish. Mary herself married John Joscelyne in 1779, a blacksmith from White Notley who had travelled to Leigh to set up in his trade. It is said that Mary and John first met at the May fair at St Clements, Leigh.

While Mary had happily married, her brother James had taken to the high seas, eventually becoming Second Lieutenant to Lord Nelson. It's James Woodward's connection to the admiral that saw him offer his childhood home, Southchurch Lawn, now Alleyne Court School, to the high profile couple as a refuge for the birth. With secrecy of the utmost importance, what could have been more natural than for James to ask his sister to attend Emma Hamilton in her capacity as a trained midwife? With Mary assisting, Emma was delivered of a baby girl, baptised Emma Seacole after the attending ship's surgeon. Once the birth was over, it is said that a stranger 'entered the room wearing a patch over one eye and with an empty sleeve to his jacket'. He looked at the baby, said nothing to the midwife, and then left the room. Despite there being an entry in the register of St Mary's, Prittlewell, it is said that the child did not survive.

What has survived is a diary written by Mary Joscelyne's daughter Charlotte, the great-great-great-grandmother of Clare Harvey, whose family history I have been privy to. Charlotte's writing hints at a secret her father, John Joscelyne, was prepared only to tell on his deathbed. The secret never was told as one day, 'as he walked across Hadleigh Fields in the noon-day sun, his blood turned to water and he died out of his mind'.

Speculation about his secret has thrown up many possibilities. It could be the fact that his son, Mary's brother William, was incarcerated in a French jail for two years, accused of spying before escaping with information that would turn events in the French war. More telling perhaps is the sudden appearance of the name Emma in Joscelyne's family records around 1804, plus the addition of the name 'Hamilton', which began to feature in Joscelyne family trees around that time. Was the death of baby Emma part of an elaborate hoax to mask a national scandal and save a gentlewoman's reputation? If so, what better ruse than to adopt her into the Joscelynes of White Notley, who to this day keep the secret of 'a gentlewoman's distress' as close to their hearts as did Mary, the nineteenth-century Essex midwife who helped bring the child into the world.

7

SAINTS AND SINNERS

ST OSYTH

St Osyth is perhaps Essex's most famous saint, and the place where she died is renowned for its holy sweet-water spring. The daughter of Frithewald and Walburga, who were rulers of East Anglia and among the first to convert to Christianity, she was brought up as a pious child. When the time came for her to marry, her parents betrothed her to the son of King Sebert, Prince Sighere, a good Christian and a man of whom Osyth approved.

Unfortunately, history tells us that young Sighere was also an avid hunter and at the wedding feast when a fine white stag roamed into view, he was unable to resist and gave chase. When he returned, Osyth had disappeared; her patience sorely tested, she had gone in search of a nunnery to which to dedicate herself. Though Sighere tried to make amends, Osyth was adamant, so by way of expressing his regret Sighere gave his virgin bride the village of Chich. Here Osyth founded her own nunnery and lived many years in peace and prayer until the holy place was set upon by marauding Danes. Breaking into the nunnery, these wolves of the north sea desecrated and plundered and were intent on debauching the women therein, but Osyth stood her ground. As Osyth was unwilling to submit to their sexual demands, nor deny her religion as ordered, the chief called for her head to be cut off, something one of his men did there and then. It is said that she immediately picked up her head and walked three furlongs, before, finally, she fell down dead. It is also said that where she fell there sprung a holy well and that place is known as nun's wood to this day.

Legend states that Osyth's head was recovered and kept in a silver casket in the nunnery she founded until it was lost in Henry VIII's Dissolution of the Monasteries. Another explanation of the miracle is that her head was never actually severed but her throat was cut and she had managed to crawl some distance before she actually perished.

St Osyth was formerly called 'Chich', but takes its present name from Osyth, the daughter of Frithwald who built a nunnery here, of which she was the first abbess. (*Robert Hallmann*)

ANNE LINE, SAINT (1567–1601)

Born at Dunmow, Essex, as Anne Higham. Hanged on 27 February 1601. Beatified 15 December 1929 by Pope Pius XI. Canonised by Pope Paul VI. Patron Saint of childless people, converts and widows.

Anne Heigham was the second daughter of Sir William Heigham and his wife Ann Allen, and grew up with her siblings in Dunmow, at a time when it was dangerous to be Catholic. Despite the promise of religious tolerance, Elizabeth I still managed to persecute great sections of the Catholic population, not for their religion but for their treason. Ann was not born Catholic. Her family were strict Calvinists, but while still a teenager she and her brother William converted to the 'true faith' and were consequently disinherited by their father.

In 1585, Anne married Roger Line of Ringwood, Hampshire. A man of means and good family, he too had been disinherited by his family for becoming a recusant. Refusal to give up the Catholic faith was a punishable offence incurring penalties such as social exclusion, deprivation of civil rights, heavy fines, imprisonment, and exile. It wasn't long after the couple had married that Anne's husband and brother were arrested for their religious activities and banished from the realm. Anne never saw her husband again. He lived out the rest of his life in Flanders where he received a small allowance from the King of Spain, part of which he sent regularly to his wife. He died in 1594 aged only twenty-eight.

With her husband exiled, Anne lost her home and succumbed to ill health, but her Catholicism had grown stronger with time and when John Gerard, a leading Jesuit missionary, asked her if she would take the risk of becoming housekeeper of a secret residence for priests that he was establishing, Anne readily accepted. Being an educated woman, Anne kept the house's accounts, taught catechism, embroidered vestments, and became fondly known to the grateful priests as 'Mrs Martha'. Feeling more and more that she had found a vocation, she also now took private vows of poverty, chastity, and obedience.

When Father John Gerard was captured and imprisoned in April 1597, Anne moved location to avoid arrest herself and to continue to protect those that needed her.

On Candlemas Day, 1601, Anne invited a large number of Catholics to attend Mass in her house, but the authorities discovered the gathering and, though the priest who officiated at the mass escaped, Anne and many of the congregation were arrested. Anne was brought before Lord Chief Justice Popham at the Old Bailey on February 26. She was so weak that she had to be carried into court in a chair. The charge against her was that of harbouring a priest, a 'treasonable act'. When asked by the court if she thought herself guilty of the crime of receiving a priest she replied in a loud voice, 'My lords, nothing grieves me more but that I could not receive a thousand more!'

Those prosecuting Anne failed to make a case against her as the priest she was charged with harbouring had not been found. Nevertheless, the judge directed the jury to find her guilty, and she was condemned to a traitor's death of being hung, drawn and quartered, though being a woman she was spared the latter two. On 27 February 1601, Anne Line was hanged on the scaffold at Tyburn, immediately before two Catholic priests. She had spent her last hours in peaceful prayer, and at Tyburn she repeated what she had said at her trial: 'I am sentenced to die for harbouring a Catholic priest, and so far I am from repenting for having so done, that I wish, with all my soul, that where I have entertained one, I could have entertained a thousand.' With that she kissed the gallows that would fulfil her wish to die for Christ. One of the priests waiting to be hanged kissed her hand while her body was still hanging, saying, 'Oh blessed Mrs Line, who has now happily received thy reward, thou art gone before us, but we shall quickly follow thee to bliss, if it please the Almighty.'

Anne Dacre, Countess of Arundel, retrieved Anne's body and held a clandestine funeral for the woman who had helped so many with no thought of her own safety. Anne Line was the only woman in the years 1590 to 1603 to be executed in England for helping priests. In 1970, she was canonised, 370 years after her death.

WITCHES

Every old woman with a wrinkled face, a furrowed brow, a hairy lip, a gobber tooth, a squint eye, a squeaking voice or scolding tongue, having a rugged coat on her back, a skull-cap on her head, a spindle in her hand and a dog or cat by her side, is not only suspect but pronounced for a witch.

(John Gaule in *Select Cases of Conscience*, his condemnation of
Matthew Hopkins)

Of those mentioned in the 'Gaol Delivery' of Colchester Castle, 10 July 1592, ten male prisoners were to be hanged, six burned in the hand for theft, seven were to be whipped for petty larceny, Randal Duckworthe was to stand in the pillory in the market (of any town) with a paper on his head for speaking scandalous words, and Frances Andrews was to be remanded for being pregnant. Agnes Draper, however, was accused of 'witchcraft'.

The discovery of a possible witch burial in 1921 in St Osyth. Iron rivets have been driven into the knees and elbows to prevent the 'witch' from rising from the grave.

Essex has long been known as the Witch County. At the height of the persecutions by Matthew Hopkins, the so-called Witchfinder General, Essex could claim the dubious honour of having hanged no less than nineteen so-called 'witches' on one day. Witchcraft was a charge so nebulous it could be brought against anyone, particularly if you were old, female, lived alone, and had earned the scorn or envy of your fellow villagers. It was not exclusive to the poor; those with an axe to grind also rid themselves of the rich and troublesome this way. For wasn't witchcraft one of the charges brought before Anne Boleyn when Henry VIII wished to divorce her?

In times of upheaval and social change there were many means by which women were kept under control. 'Scolds bridles' were used to silence women who upset the public order and quiet with their nagging, while the 'cucking stool' (also known as the 'ducking stool'), another old English 'engine of correction', was a water punishment designed to humiliate and, for the spectators, entertain.

As early as 1424 in South Hanningfield, the lord of the manor complained of the lack of repair to the stocks and cucking stool; it appears that water punishments were a mandatory form of deterrent. Witham Quarter Session Rolls of 1575 informs us that a certain 'James Cooke sells ale without a license and they do not have a cucking stool there'. An Inquisition taken before the village constable Robert Bretton in Doddinghurst in 1573 reports that their cucking stool was 'in decay'. Belchamp St Paul had a cucking stool in 1595 along with a tumbril and pillory. Similar instruments of reprimand could be found in Aveley, a small village a few miles east of Rainham and close to the Thames and Essex marshes. There was a 'cukkyngstolfeld' (cucking stool field) mentioned in documents concerning Chipping (Saffron) Walden in 1440. Later, a cottage in Cucking Stool End (17 feet long and 15 feet wide) is mentioned in land transactions of 1714. As late as 1819, court papers of Maldon record a local man, Silvanus Horton, aged eighty-five years, saying he remembers a cucking stool at the Hythe 'which was locked down with a chain'.

Cucking stools were a common punishment for witchcraft, the ultimate charge a religiously and socially divided society could impose upon a woman. It is known that when Elizabeth I became Queen of England she encouraged the seeking out of witches. When she stayed at St Osyth, Essex, in 1561, and again in 1579, her host Lord John D'Arcy, Justice of the Peace in St Osyth, took it upon himself to rid the village and surrounding areas of witches. He used the same persuasive techniques as Matthew Hopkins, and by all accounts he was a successful witch-hunter. A book in the Bodleian Library, Oxford, contains 'A true and just recorde of the enformation, examination and confession of all witches taken at St Osees', condemning two local women, Elizabeth Bennet and Ursula Kemp. With the case against them based solely upon the accusations of neighbours and even Ursula's own son Thomas, the two women were found guilty and hanged in 1582. A man digging in his garden at 37 Mill Street, St Osyth, early in the last century, came upon two skeletons whose main joints were bound, elbow to elbow, wrist to wrist. The skeletons are believed to be the remains of Elizabeth and Ursula, buried head to foot and nailed down to prevent them escaping their joint grave.

With scientific explanation for natural events centuries away, the supernatural was blamed for sickness, stillbirth, and loss of livestock. Assizes were usually held at Chelmsford. It is estimated that between 1566 and 1645, some ninety supposed witches were sent to the scaffold.

The first major English trial for witchcraft took place at Chelmsford in 1566. The accused were Agnes Waterhouse, her daughter Joan, and Elizabeth Francis, all from Hatfield Peverell. The three were linked by their possession in turn of a cat named Satan, a resourceful beast that spoke in a strange, hollow voice and occasionally assumed the shapes of a toad and a black dog. According to the prosecution, Satan killed a man who refused to respond to Elizabeth's advances, and later gave her a husband and child. The cat was then given to the Waterhouses for whom it spoilt butter and cheese, drowned a neighbour's cows, and bewitched a man to death. While Elizabeth Francis only received a year's imprisonment, she was eventually

The public hanging of three 'witches' in Chelmsford, Essex, in 1589.

accused again and hanged for witchcraft in 1579. Joan Waterhouse was released, but her mother, confessing to all the charges, was hanged.

The most famous witch trials are well documented, but not all accusations of witchcraft brought the woman to a major trial. To be indicted and found 'not guilty' was to be doubted for life; the women concerned were made into objects of future suspicion and derision. Many women charged with witchcraft died or languished in Chelmsford Gaol. In December 1595, Thomas Wiseman of Wighborough and his servant John Vickers gave evidence against Faith Somer, who had been accused of witchcraft. However, the trial was dismissed and John Vickers was told to keep the peace toward a fellow yeoman's wife. A misunderstanding perhaps? The result of a vindictive mind or thwarted advances? In the battle of the sexes, an accusation of witchcraft was certainly a weapon a man could call upon.

In 1560, Joan Haddon of Witham was tried as a common witch for fraudulently receiving sums of money from a man and his wife after bewitching them; she was pardoned. Other cases thrown out of court were Elizabeth Lowys or Lowes of Great Waltham for supposedly bewitching John Wodley, aged three months, and Anne Vale of White Roding for the death of husbandman John Berdes' pigs. Joan Gibson of Messing was a spinster accused of bewitching a windmill belonging to George Clarke, and Alice Gardiner of Boreham was brought to trial for 'giving counsell to a witche'. All were found not guilty and freed, but Agnes Coples of Romford, who called 'Gentrie's wife a witch, in anger', was ordered to do a penance.

The last execution for witchcraft was in 1682, the last trial was in 1712, and the law was repealed in 1736. Some witchcraft beliefs, however, die hard, and still persist in parts of Essex to this day. Witches are still believed to be living in Canewdon; and there is a legend that one witch dies and another is born every time a stone falls from the church tower. Given that the tower is one of the largest in Essex, it may be an eternity before Canewdon is free from witches.

8

WARRIOR WOMEN

BOUDICCA, A WOMAN SCORNED

A Briton woman of the royal family and possessed of greater intelligence than often belongs to women. In stature she was very tall, in appearance most terrifying, in the glance of her eye most fierce, and her voice was harsh; a great mass of the tawniest hair fell to her hips; around her neck was a large golden necklace and she wore a tunic of divers colours over which a thick mantle was fastened with a brooch. This was her invariable attire.

(Cassius Dio)

While not strictly an Essex girl, Boudicca certainly left her mark on the county. That mark is known in archaeological circles as 'Boudicca's Destruction Horizon', but to lesser mortals who dig down deep enough in Colchester, London, or St Albans, it is the distinctive line of soot and charcoal that is a permanent reminder of the British revolt against the Romans.

That Boudicca was a warrior queen at all is not unusual. The Roman Empire was well aware of the ferocity of women in tribal warfare, mostly from experiencing invasions across their own borders. Written after one such invasion, Roman historian Marcus Borealis reported:

The women of the Celtic tribes are bigger and stronger than our Roman women. This is most likely due to their natures as well as their peculiar fondness for all things martial and robust. The flaxen haired maidens of the north are trained in sports and war while our gentle ladies are content to do their womanly duties and thus are less powerful than most young girls from Gaul and the hinterlands.

An unidentified Roman soldier of the same historical period gives another testament:

> A Celtic woman is often the equal of any Roman man in hand-to-hand combat. She is as beautiful as she is strong. Her body is comely but fierce. The physiques of our Roman women pale in comparison.

In retrospect, it should have been clear that upsetting a Celtic queen would only end in bloodshed.

For a woman, Boudicca seems to have possessed great military knowledge, which became apparent during the preparations and war council assemblies she addressed before her forces took on the might of Rome. Boudicca would have received her training and education, learnt about Celtic traditions, local gods, and customs of her tribe by spending her early years under the guardianship of another aristocratic family. The customary exchange of children between different families and tribes was an important way of cementing friendships, keeping good relations between local families, passing on their ancestor's knowledge (for they did not have the written word), and thus preserving Celtic culture as well as establishing loyalty.

Popular belief has Boudicca's birth date around AD 30, and it is thought that she married around the age of eighteen. With her husband, Prasutagus, at least a decade older than her, it is possible she could have even been his second wife. Two girls were a result of this amicable marriage which ended only when Prasutagus died in about AD 60/61. This left Boudicca, now about thirty years of age, the temporary leader of the Icini until a new king could be selected by the council of tribal chieftains. It also left her extremely wealthy. Unlike women of other societies, Celtic women were entitled to a great many privileges. They could inherit property from their fathers and husbands and become rich and powerful rulers in their own right, like Queen Cartimandua of the Brigantes tribe.

Prasutagus' will left half of his land and estate to the Romans as part of an earlier agreement that allowed him to remain king after the Roman invasion, and the other half to Boudicca and their two daughters. Roman law disregarded Boudicca's inheritance, fearful of creating too many women of wealth and power in their new province. On the pretext that grants, once given to the British tribes as gestures of goodwill from the Emperor Claudius, were now in fact loans repayable to the new Emperor Nero, Roman officials demanded Prasutagus' widow repay her debt, plus interest. When Boudicca protested her inability to pay the huge amounts, Rome decided to recover the debt by force. In the words of the Roman historian Tacitus:

Kingdom and household were plundered like prizes of war, the one by Roman officers, the other by Roman slaves. As a beginning his (Prasutagus's) widow was flogged and her daughters raped.

The treatment meted out to Boudicca and her daughters – and to their people, many of whom were evicted and made slaves – turned the previously pragmatic Iceni into rebels. Beaten but unbowed, Boudicca fled to the tribe's centre at Thetford where she raised an army and led them south towards the colonia at Camulodunum (Colchester). Boudicca had chosen her target out of pure revenge. Camulodunum was the Roman's capital town complete with a senate building, shops, a theatre, and a temple dedicated to the late Emperor Claudius, conqueror of Britain. The Romans had forcibly ejected the natives off this land and had confiscated their property in order to build the settlement for their veteran soldiers and their families, subjecting the local Britons to cruel punishments if they dared object. The soldiers of the Colchester garrison were also the ones responsible for the atrocities done to Boudicca and her daughters.

Boudicca's forces approached Colchester, meeting no opposition. Most of the Roman military forces in Britain were engaged in a concerted attempt to wipe out the druids on Anglesey; Camulodunum had, at best, a skeleton defence force. When news of Boudicca's travelling hordes reached the town, the locals pressed Catus Decianus, the man responsible for triggering the uprising, to provide military assistance. He mustered barely 200 troops before fleeing to Gaul in fear of his life.

When Boudicca reached the colonia her army fell upon the place in an outrage of aggression and destruction. She was ruthless. The joint forces of the Icini and the Trinovantes tribe showed no mercy, forcing their way through the defending soldiers' token resistance. Nothing and no one was spared as thousands of screaming, blue-painted warriors massacred 30,000 men, women, and children. Even those sheltering inside the Temple of Claudius were killed where they stood; Britons scaled the walls and dismantled the roof, dropping it down on to them. As testament to this total destruction, Colchester museum today contains the tombstone of a Roman cavalryman, Longinus Sdapezematygus, which was defaced when Boudicca razed the colonia.

Boudicca's forces probably stayed among the ruins of Britain's Roman capital to celebrate and divide up the spoils, though it was against Celtic religion to keep booty for themselves. Profiteering from the proceeds of stolen loot was considered a sin punishable by death and so plunder was usually buried to placate the gods, perhaps explaining why so many hoards containing Roman artefacts have been unearthed over the centuries. After a few days, and still filled with bloodlust, they headed south for Londinium.

With only 30,000 inhabitants, Londinium was a fairly new settlement. Goods and slaves were exported here, while imports were unloaded amid noise and bustle. Suetonius Paulinus, the commander of the Roman forces, arrived with his cavalry and had two options in the face of the danger that was approaching him: fight or flight. Knowing how Camulodunum had been devastated and that the numbers of Boudicca's warriors grew daily, he opted for the latter.

Outnumbered, he could still have mustered what soldiers he had and defended the town as best he could. But, by deciding instead to strengthen his numbers and engage the rebel queen at full strength elsewhere, he delivered Londinium into the unforgiving hands of fate.

When Boudicca's forces arrived, Londinium was almost deserted, and those that stayed were not spared. Cassius Dio describes what the rebels did to the locals who were left:

> The city's most distinguished women were hung up naked, their breasts cut off and sewn into their mouths, before being impaled on stakes.

When the Thames was running red with blood, the rebels torched London, burning many alive in their homes.

Once Londinium had been ransacked, the rebels made for Verulamium, now St Albans.

By the time Boudicca arrived, the town was deserted, the locals having taken everything of value with them. Boudicca's rage was still vent upon the town, but her army was wearying and Verulamium proved to be the last of her victories. Boudicca fought the final battle of her revolt against the amassed legions of Seutonius Paulinus somewhere in the Midlands. It is not known exactly where, but many historians believe the battle to have been at Mancetter in Warwickshire. Though she believed wars were won with sinew, skill, and personal strategy, her beliefs were no match for the brute force and iron discipline of the Romans. In a single volley of Roman javelins, thousands of her lightly armoured, loyal warriors were slain. Despite furious hand to hand fighting, the Celts never recovered the field.

There are many theories about what happened to the warrior queen after the battle. Some say she took poison rather than suffer the ignominy of being taken to Rome and paraded through the streets. Others say she simply disappeared with her daughters. There is a rumour that Boudicca is buried beneath Platform 8 at King's Cross Station in London, while in 2006 Birmingham archaeologists claimed they had found her grave in

A nineteenth-century ideal of the Celtic queen Boudicca. This statue by Thomas Thorneycroft (1902) stands near Westminster Pier, London.

King's Norton, next to McDonald's. Wherever she rests, there is no denying that she was a woman who gave the Romans a run for their money, at a time when Rome did not venerate womanhood. Women were not even recognised in Roman law and it was accepted that if a man caught his wife in adultery, 'you can kill her with impunity; she, however, cannot dare to lay a finger on you'.

As Boudicca's history was written by Roman historians long after her demise, we have become used to the biased account of events we have been left. But even Tacitus credits this Celtic queen with the courage to take on the full force of the Roman Empire.

Boudicca, in a chariot, with her two daughters before her, drove through the ranks. She harangued the different nations in their turn: 'This', she said, 'is not the first time that the Britons have been led to battle by a woman.' But now she did not come to boast the pride of a long line of ancestry, nor even to recover her kingdom and the plundered wealth of her family. She took the field, like the meanest among them, to assert the cause of public liberty, and to seek revenge for her body seamed with ignominious stripes, and her two daughters infamously ravished: 'From the pride and arrogance of the Romans nothing is sacred; all are subject to violation; the old endure the scourge, and the virgins are deflowered. But the vindictive gods are now at hand. A Roman legion dared to face the warlike Britons: with their lives they paid for their rashness; those who survived the carnage of that day, lie poorly hid behind their entrenchments, meditating nothing but how to save themselves by an ignominious flight. From the din of the preparation, and the shouts of the British army, the Romans, even now, shrink back with terror. What will be their case when the assault begins? Look round, and view your numbers. Behold the proud display of warlike spirits, and consider the motives for which we draw the avenging sword. On this spot we must either conquer, or die with glory. There is no alternative. Though a woman, my resolution is fixed: the men, if they please, may survive with infamy, and live in bondage.'

(Tacitus *Annals*, chapter 35)

AMAZONS AT BRENTWOOD

Even the ordinary Essex woman is not afraid to defend or stand up for what she thinks is right when pushed to it. From 1577, there exists a single record of an incident that saw several spinsters of the parish of Brentwood raise a riot when the new lord of the manor, Wistan Browne, saw fit to close Burntwood Chapel. So opposed to his intention to pull the building down, Thomasina Tyler, Anna Woodall, Margaret Banester, Alice Greatheade, Priscilla Prior, Margaret Bayford, Mary May, Alice Degon, Dorothea Woodall and twenty-one others occupied the steeple, and the graveyard, before dragging school teacher Richard Brooke out of the chancel and 'beating him'. After this they then shut themselves in chapel with weapons ready to defend themselves against the servants of the sheriff.

These weapons were no kitchen utensils. In an account of the incident, they are listed as: 'five pitchforks, bills, a piked staff, two hot spits, three bows, nine arrows, an axe, a great hammer, two kettles of hot water, and

The thirteenth-century chapel of St Thomas-a-Becket in Brentwood, where in 1577 several 'spinsters of the parish' raised a riot to stop the lord of the manor from closing it. The building remained in use as a chapel until 1835, and it was then used as a boys' school until 1869 when it was mostly demolished. (*Essex Record Office*)

a great whetstone.' The chapel was successfully held by the women for the remainder of the day and they eventually disbanded, but not before representatives of the law had tried to commit Thomasina Tyler to prison. This was thwarted due to local support for the women, namely by the yeoman John Myntor of Burntwood, who refused to obey the order to arrest Thomasina, and by the labourer Henry Dalley of Burntwood, who 'forcably [sic] with violence' hindered the authorities in her apprehension. As it turned out, other people had petitioned against the new landlord, and though Browne at that time was the sheriff of Essex, he was still to be summoned before the Privy Council and called to account. Justice swung in the women's favour with Browne considered mainly to blame for the trouble. As a result, the Essex magistrate dealt gently with the rioters.

ANNE CARTER (d. 1629)

Words will not fill the belly nor clothe the backe.

In the seventeenth century, the long-suffering 'Essex girl' was to show her disapproval of events surrounding her more than in any other period of Essex history. The latter part of that century has been called an age of enlightenment, yet the first fifty years saw more religious and social upheaval than in previous centuries, and nowhere more so than in Essex. Women left the county in pursuit of religious freedom, following their husbands into a dangerous new world. Of those that stayed, many had to fight for their very existence in the face of bad harvests and economic policies that often saw them on the brink of starvation.

Anne Carter of Maldon was one such Essex girl. Information on her life is scarce, but as with most women in history, if they are mentioned at all it must mean that what they are mentioned for is noteworthy. Anne's name appears in 1629, alongside that of Anne Spearman, Elizabeth Sturgion and Dorothy Berry, all of Maldon, in a document that reveals they were 'examined' for their participation in what has since become known as the Maldon Grain Riots. Though the outcome suggests otherwise, these women, and Anne in particular, had sought nothing more than justice for a grievance, which had admittedly culminated in civil unrest. They simply wanted to feed their families; the state of desperation that surrounded the depression of the cloth trade in Essex during the first quarter of the seventeenth century was a powder keg waiting for a flame.

We have no dates for Anne's birth or marriage, but we know that her husband, John Carter, was a 'butcher of Maldon' and therefore a tradesman. There is a tiny glimpse of Anne's character encapsulated in an answer she gave to an alderman, possibly in a local court of law. Perhaps she was there to pay the one shilling (5 pence) fine for non-attendance at church as her impudent reply to Alderman Rudland was that she'd be prepared to go to church on Sunday if he would find someone to do her housework for her. Whether her words portray her as feisty or a woman with contempt for the law, it nevertheless suggests she was someone prepared to stand her ground. It also suggests a woman oppressed by the constantly changing religious laws and, of course, poverty.

We know for certain that Anne lived through the reign of James I (1603-1625), a pedantic and unpopular monarch believing in the 'Divine Right of Kings', an ideal passed on to his son, Charles I. This confrontational approach soon led to the suspension of Parliament on many occasions – a direct result of Charles not getting his own way. His rule was a far cry from the diplomacy and statesmanship of his predecessor Elizabeth I.

Anne would have felt the full impact of these two monarchs' economic policies, especially when harvests were bad and she and her husband would have been liable for a myriad of fines and taxes levied when the monarchy needed money. She definitely would have felt the tensions throughout her home town when Irish troops were billeted in Maldon and Witham in 1628 as punishment for the townspeople having resisted the king's latest 'Forced Loan'.

Local government could do little to curb the soldiers' quarrelsome and loutish behaviour, and soon feelings of dissatisfaction and dissent began to influence the uneasy truce the townsfolk had with the immigrant Dutch. This community, which had settled in Essex's northern towns of Colchester, Braintree, Coggeshall, Bocking and Halsted, and whose cloth making had given work to some 60,000 local spinners, weavers and combers, could no longer supply work due to decreased demand for their goods abroad. In the grip of another bad harvest, and with record numbers of people petitioning the justices of the peace for poor relief, anti-Dutch feeling had rarely been so high.

In all fairness, the local Justices of the Peace had dealt with matters arising out of those difficult times leniently. They raised poor relief from more affluent citizens, and they even borrowed grain from as far away as Norfolk. They used their knowledge of the law where they could and sometimes, as in the cases of men such as Lord Maynard and Lord Riche, they used their own means to do what they could to alleviate the people's suffering. Matters were raised to magistrate level when, in March 1629, the people's – and especially the women's – anger finally spilled over.

The Maldon Grain Riots were women's riots. Wives who were themselves 'pinched with want and famine' could no longer accept their husbands' diminishing wages, and mothers who cried out that 'words will not fill the belly nor clothe the backe,' could not and would not stand by and see their children starve. Earlier, in January, a flurry of unrest in the south of the county had seen mostly men, armed with pitchforks, manage to halt a shipment of grain by seizing cartloads of it headed for the river Thames. But in March it was some 140 women, drawn from the towns of Heybridge and Witham, who, together with their sisters from Maldon, gathered in Maldon's market square under the alleged leadership of Anne Carter. The women boarded a Flemish merchant ship which was 'emptying Maldon market' of desperately needed grain, and at Anne's insistence the ship's crew filled their aprons and bonnets with grain which they took away to feed their families. Perhaps the crew themselves were sympathetic.

Another riot followed two months later. This time a group of two to three hundred weavers from Bocking, Braintree and Witham mustered in Maldon market square. Roused by the alleged words, 'Come my brave

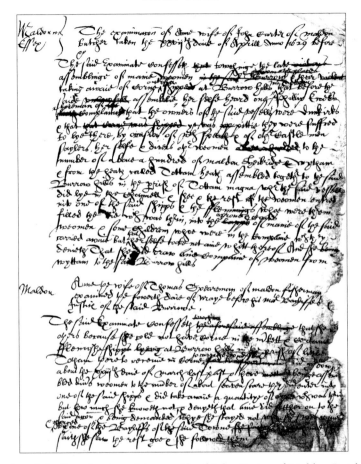

'Transcript of the Examination of Anne wife of John Carter of Maldon Butcher', dated 1629.

The examination of Anne wife of John Carter of Maldon butcher taken the 28th day of April anno 1629 ... the said examinate confesseth touching the late assembling of many women and their taking away of corn out of the ships at Burrow Hills in Totham that before the said assembly, herard one Philip Ewdes a hoyman of Lee complain that the owners of the said vessel were Dunkirks [Dunkirk merchants] and that it was pity they were suffered to lie there, by occaision of which speech and other men sailors, herself and divers other women to the number of above a hundred of Maldon, Heybridge and Witham and from the heath called Totham heath assembled together to the said Burrow Hills in the parish of greater Totham where the said vessels did lie in the channel and she and the rest of the women entered into one of the said ships, and the Flemmings who were therein filled the rye which was therein into the aprons and coats of many of the women and some children who were in the company which they carried away but that herself took not any whit thereof. And she denieth that she did draw any company of women from Witham to the said Burrow Hills.

For her part in the Maldon Grain riots, Anne Carter was made an example of, and boys of Maldon! I will be your leader for we shall not want for bread' from their self-appointed 'Captain', Anne Carter, they marched to Burrow Hills, a deep-water channel outside of Maldon in the parishes of Great and Little Totham. Here, fifteen quarters of rye were looted from ships bound for Europe, one ship being forced to pay a twenty-pound 'fine' for its freedom. Fearing greater uprisings to follow, local government issued a commission of 'Oyer and Terminer' (the setting up of a local court with the power to summon a jury and decide cases), which proceeded to apprehend the rioters. Among those 'examined' before the bailiffs was Dorothy Berry, who, when questioned what had prompted her to take such action, gave the heartfelt reply: 'the crie of the countrie and my owne want'.

Dorothy, a shepherd's wife, was questioned on 4 May 1629, as were Anne Spearman, the wife of a fisherman, and Elizabeth Sturgion, the wife of a labourer. The questions centred on who had led and encouraged them on 23 March. According to the transcript of the 'examination', neither of the women seems to have implicated Anne Carter. Her 'examination' had taken place earlier, on 28 April. She admitted that she had, with more than a hundred others, gone down to the ships at Burrow Hills. They had heard 'one Philip Ewdes, a hoyman of Lee, complain that the owners of the said vessel were Dunkirks (Dunkirk merchants) and that it was pity they were suffered to lie there.' The 'Flemmings', she said, 'filled the rye which was therein into the aprons and coats of many of the women and some children.' She denied she had taken any herself and she also denied she had led the others. Unusually ruthless for civil disturbance of this kind, it was proclaimed that four rioters were to be made examples of. Three men and one woman were hung. The woman was Anne Carter.

9

ROMANTIC ESSEX GIRLS

EDITH SWAN-NECK

One, Edith of the Swan's Neck, dwells / In a hovel poor and rude. / They named her thus, because her neck / Was once as slim and white / As any swan's – when, long ago, / She was the king's delight. / He loved and kissed, forsook, forgot, / For such is the way of men.
(From *The Battlefield of Hastings* by Heinrich Heine)

The story of Edith Swan-Neck is certainly a romantic one with real-life love and pathos. As the 'hand-fast' wife of King Harold of England, it is said it was she who identified Harold's mutilated body on the battlefield of Hastings when nobody else could. This she did by finding small 'lover's marks' known only to her. After twenty years of knowing the king intimately, this was the only way of distinguishing the Harold's corpse, in the words of a chronicler, 'among the other loathsome heaps of the unburied'. Known to all as Harold's 'old love', Edith had never been the king's wife in the eyes of the Church. But six children later and still bound together 'More danico' ('in the Danish manner'), this last act of selflessness was the least she could have done for the man she loved.

At the time of his death, Harold was forty-five years old and legally married to the widowed Ealdgyth of Mercia, sister of Edwin and Morcar, two northern Earls. It was purely a political union, perhaps borne out by the fact that on hearing of the king's death, Ealdgyth fled north back to her family. By the same token, Harold's relationship with Edith Swan-Neck – also known as Edith the Fair – had been one of a long and mutual regard. The couple had first met at Nazeing, where Harold's estates reached deep into Epping Forest and Edith lived on one of his manors. Soon after the couple became united in a 'hand-fasting' ceremony. Some say this was

Edith Swan-Neck was the only person able to identify King Harold's body after the Battle of Hastings. His 'hand-fast' wife of twenty years, she did this by finding small 'lover's marks' known only to her.

because Edith was not of high enough status to warrant a conventional marriage ceremony. Others explain that this was the preferred method of union for Germanic people. It is likely that Harold followed this method of wedding because his own mother was Danish. Today we would call it a common-law ceremony.

'Hand-Festre' is old Norse for 'to strike a bargain by joining hands'; the subsequent ritual involved the tying or binding of the right hands of the bride and groom with a cord. It usually took place for the duration of the wedding ceremony, occasionally until consummation. Typically, if the left hands were bound together, it usually denoted that the woman was the mistress. In this instance, she herself would have no claim to name, property or inheritance; however, her children would be considered as legal heirs, though second to any 'legitimate' offspring

It was agreed that the couples would live together for a year and a day as husband and wife, after which, if they were still happy together, they would agree to be married. If the couple then consummated their betrothal, they were considered married and the hand-fast legally binding. Alternatively, if no consummation took place, no marriage was considered to have taken place and one or both parties could cancel the arrangement.

Certainly Harold Godwinson and Edith's marriage was a love match, definitely consummated and thus legally binding. Edith bore her 'husband' six children, none of which were considered illegitimate by the culture at that time. One of their daughters, Gyda Haraldsdatter (also known as Gytha of Wessex) was addressed as 'Princess' and was married to the Grand Duke of Kiev, Vladimir Monomakh, thus connecting her to the kings of Denmark, Hungary and, by way of the kings of Aragon, the kings of England and France. The couple's other children were Godwin, Edmund, Magnus, Ulf, and Gunhilds.

No one can imagine the heartache Edith must have felt as she approached Senlac Hill to identify the body of her husband. If the Abbott of Hythe and twelve monks could not find the king, he must have been stripped of all insignia and mutilated beyond recognition. It is doubtful the invading Normans showed their enemy any mercies. After all, chivalry was at best a romantic idea and these men were adventurers and mercenaries. Eventually, as history would have it, barefoot in the blood and mire of the battlefield, Edith found Harold, and crying out, fell upon his body. In the words of poet Heinrich Heine:

> She kissed his brow, she kissed his mouth,
>   She clasped him close, and pressed
> Her poor lips to the bloody wounds –
>   That gaped upon his breast.

The Saxon interior of Waltham Holy Cross, the church built by King Harold where his body was reputedly taken after the Battle of Hastings. (*Robert Hallmann*)

> His shoulder stark she kisses too,
> When, searching, she discovers
> Three little scars her teeth had made
> When they were happy lovers.

Stories continue to tell us that Edith Swan-Neck took Harold back to Essex and buried him in the church he loved, Waltham Holy Cross, which he had commissioned several years before the battle. It was his dearest wish to be buried there, though modern investigation of the site has not so far confirmed the abbey as his last resting place.

FRANCES RICHE (*c.*1539–1581)

No tale of love in Essex would be complete without the tale of the independent and spirited Frances Riche of Leeze and Rochford. This tale of an eloping couple has passed into Essex folklore and still inspires the lovelorn to this day. For those unfamiliar with the story, it is one of 'derring-do' in a time when women, like children, were supposed to be seen but not heard. They were certainly not supposed to abscond from under their father's nose with the man of their dreams, especially when that man was already a widower with nine children to his name

The man in question was the handsome widower, Captain Thomas Cammock. In the Earl of Warwick's employ, he had wooed the young Frances in secret because of her parents' disapproval until one day, while in transit between Great Leeze and Rochford, Frances and Thomas took a horse and, pursued by a servant, galloped towards South Fambridge to take the ferry and escape to Maldon. In the vein of all true romance, adversity was at hand: firstly because her father had discovered their flight and given chase and was now close behind, and secondly because when they reached the bank of the River Crouch the ferry was tied up on the far side.

It was stay or swim. Though Thomas warned her against crossing, the two lovers entered the dark and stormy waters, Frances professing she would live or die with Thomas as they struggled against the tide. As their horse reached midpoint, the servant in pursuit reached the bank and his horse whinnied. Their horse, when hearing the sound, tried to return to the original bank and only with great difficulty did the lovers manage to keep it from swimming back. Having reached the north bank, they rode on to Maldon, were wedded and bedded. Lord Riche, seeing 'she had ventured her life for him,' declared 'God Bless 'em' and accepted the marriage.

It was a happy and fruitful union. Frances added two sons and eleven daughters to the four sons and five daughters Captain Cammock's first wife, Ursula, had already given him. Ursula had been well loved in the family and had, on the occasion of her father-in-law's death, been left two 'gold Angels' (20 shillings) for a ring'. An incident involving Frances a few years before her husband died suggests that she may not have been so easily accepted by some as perhaps Ursula had been. Reading through historical records concerning the families of Cammock and Tuke of Layer Marney, one detects a feeling of disharmony, and a rivalry that could have sparked the incident that found itself recorded in the Michaelmas Session Court of 1598.

Frances, along with her ten-year-old daughter Martha and servant Robert Beridge, appears to have been set upon by 'malefactors' and

Two views of North Fambridge where lovers Frances Riche and Captain Thomas Cammock reputedly swam the River Crouch rather than be parted. (*Robert Hallmann*)

'disturbers of the peace' when, on July 23, they wished to enter church to hear Divine Service. The jury heard that Elizabeth Tuke, wife of Peter Tuke, Esq., and Thomas Styse, a carpenter, had deliberately hung a lock on the Cammock family pew in order to hinder Frances. The jury also heard that it had been Elizabeth Tuke, along with her servant, who had incited the mob to obstruct her. Elizabeth then proceeded to assault Frances, tear her lawn apron, and violently withhold Mistress Cammock and her daughter from the said pew. Frances, it was said, had been 'in peril of death'.

Perhaps it was simply religious differences that led the Tukes to act in such a fashion? Or perhaps jealousy or a disagreement over property? Whatever it was, it was certainly serious enough to see Elizabeth's servant, Nathanial Beridge, a relation of Frances' servant Robert, take up against his own family. Perhaps a fateful glimpse of the future civil war?

Frances' spirit had showed itself again in the scuffle and it was she who commissioned the monument to her husband after his death. It is an impressive memorial. The twenty-five Cammocks are all portrayed in alabaster high on the east wall of the north aisle of All Saints' church. A middle aged man, Captain Cammock, is gowned and kneeling, flanked by his two wives, their faces turned towards him, while the faces of children of all ages look up from below.

NELL GWYNN (1650–1687)

But first the basket her fair arm did suit,
Laden with pippins and Hesperian fruit;
This first step raised, to the wondering pit she sold
The lovely fruit smiling with streaks of gold.

For so many of us, Nell Gwyn is the archetypal strumpet, that woman of easy virtue who climbs the social ladder enjoying every dishonourable moment. But to others, 'pretty witty Nell' is a romantic figure. After all, the dictionary definition of 'romance' is given as 'an ardent emotional attachment' and that's certainly what she shared with that most merry of monarchs, King Charles II. Unlike the king's other mistresses, Nell was completely faithful.

Nell's connection with Essex is tenuous, but she did, on many occasions, accompany the king on his travels into this county. Here the royal party would hawk and hunt and afterwards lodge at various venues – in particular New Hall, Boreham. In 1517, the estate had belonged to Thomas Boleyn. It was then purchased by the crown and renamed Beaulieu after Henry VIII had refurbished it in brick, but it was a name that did not outlast the century.

Eleanor Gwyn by Sir Peter Lely. Appointed Principal Painter to the King in 1661, Lely was the dominant court and society portraitist of the reign of Charles II. One of his favourite subjects was 'pretty, witty Nell'.

For many years the home of Mary Tudor, New Hall passed to the Earl of Sussex, the Duke of Buckingham, and Oliver Cromwell who procured the estate for five shillings. At the restoration in 1660, George Monck, first Duke of Albermarle, became the owner and Charles II and his court were invited to stay on numerous occasions. It was here that Nell entertained her king by playing in Shakespeare's *The Merry Wives of Windsor*.

To put the phenomenon that was 'Nell', or Eleanor Gwynn, into context, is to briefly describe the life and the England into which she was born. She was born in 1650, almost exactly a year after the execution of Charles I had left the nation both shocked and bewildered. With the Puritans now in power, theatres were closed, maypoles forbidden, and public entertainments and holidays banned, as was dancing, singing, and playing musical instruments. Even wrestling, leaping, running and 'unnecessary' walking (e.g. walking for pleasure) were denied to the common people. Children were given preposterous names such as Abstinence, Forsaken, Ashes, Repentance and Kill-Sin, while adultery was made a capital offence. Puritanism was threatening to dismantle society and under its new regime a woman's status became little better than that of a child. For people everywhere, there was a strong feeling that the end of the world was approaching.

England was 'restored' with the accession to the throne of Charles II in 1660, when Nell was just ten years old. Simple pleasures were reinstated, and theatres – those symbols of pleasure and decadence condemned by the Puritans – re-opened with women now at legal liberty to act upon the stage. One of Charles' early acts as king was to license the formation of two acting companies; in 1663 the King's Company, led by Thomas Killigrew, opened a new playhouse, the Theatre in Bridges Street (later rebuilt and renamed the Theatre Royal at Drury Lane).

Mary Meggs, a former prostitute nicknamed 'Orange Moll' and a friend of Madam Gwyn (Nell's mother), had been granted the license to 'vend, utter and sell oranges, lemons, fruit, sweetmeats and all manner of fruiterers and confectioners wares' within the theatre. Orange Moll hired Nell and her older sister Rose as 'orange-girls', selling the small, sweet 'china' oranges to the audience inside the theatre for sixpence each. Whereas her sister went on to become the wife of a highwayman, within a year the pretty Nell had risen from vendor to actress; her good looks, strong clear voice and lively wit caught the eye of the owner of the theatre, and yet she was still only fourteen. But looks alone were not enough and she realised she had to be both hardworking and clever. Restoration plays were short, with up to fifty productions played out over a nine-month season from September to June. Such a workload was no mean task; Nell had to commit thousands of lines to memory despite being illiterate.

Many plays of the day, such as *The Maiden Queen*, contained breeches roles, where the actresses appeared in men's clothes, which highlighted their figures. As a result, theatres often lost their actresses to the aristocracy who kept them as mistresses. Young Nell was no exception. In 1667, Nell Gwyn became involved with Lord Buckhurst, namely Charles Sackville, but a year later she embarked upon a romance with the king. This came about after Nell was left to pay a supper bill for the king, his brother, her companion, and herself, after Charles discovered he had no money about him. Witty as ever, Nell had declared, 'but this is the poorest company I ever was in!' By the summer of 1668, Nell's affair with the king was well known and her notoriety pulled in large crowds at the playhouses and prompted playwrights to create new roles for her.

King Charles II had a considerable number of mistresses through his life, both short affairs and committed arrangements. Nell on the other hand referred to Charles as 'Charles the third', he being the last of only three men she had ever had a lasting relationship with. Their fascination with each other meant that they were lovers for sixteen years, within which time Nell gave birth to two sons by her royal lover, one raised into the aristocracy, the second dying young at school in France. King Charles himself died on 6 February 1685; his last wish of his brother was that he 'Let not poor Nelly starve'. James honoured this request, eventually paying off most of Gwyn's debts and awarding her a pension of £1500 a year. In March 1687, Nell suffered a stroke that left her paralysed on one side. In May, a second stroke left her confined to bed in her Pall Mall house where she made out her will on 9 July. Nell Gwyn died on 14 November 1687, at ten in the evening, less than three years after the king's death. She was thirty-seven years old.

Far from being empty-headed, 'pretty, witty Nell' was admired by the diarist Samuel Pepys, who had first coined the description, and was also a friend of the poet John Dryden. She was genuinely popular with the English public as she never claimed to be anything other than what she was, and it was her wit that endeared her to them. One day as she drove through the streets, her coach encountered a mob intent on delaying her as they took her for the Duchess of Portsmouth, the king's Catholic mistress. Above the noise, Nell was heard to defuse the situation by declaring, 'Good people, you are mistaken, I am the Protestant Whore'. Similarly, when she found her coachman fighting another man who had called her a whore, she broke up the fight, saying 'I am a whore, find something else to fight about!'

Nell lived two years longer than Charles, his death being the only reason their close relationship ended. In her will she was generous to her servants and nurses and 'laid out £20 yearly for the releasing of poor debtors from prison every Christmas day', a legacy prompted by her years of plight from which the king had generously saved her, and influenced by the belief that her father had ended his days in Newgate. She is also said to have been the one to persuade the king to build the Chelsea Hospital in London for ex-servicemen, an institution praised in this contemporary account:

> There were old men who had fought at Edge Hill and Marston Moor, and younger ones who could show that they had bled at Naseby or at Worcester. The Restoration had witnessed the establishment of a standing army, and many of Cromwell's Ironsides filling the ranks of the Coldstream Guards and Oxford Blues were now unfit for active service, and younger men were required to fill their places. What was to become of the veterans when their pay was gone? Their trade had been war, and their pay never sufficient for more than their immediate wants. But for Chelsea Hospital they might have starved.

CATHERINE 'KITTY' CANHAM (1720–1752)

A young and lovely woman, with a sad wistful expression in her soft hazel eyes, her brown hair slightly powdered, and falling in curls round her neck and shoulders.

The life and times of Kitty Canham are already well documented. Referred to as the 'Beautiful Bigamist', she was born in 1720 and after a brief spell as the wife of a clergyman, gave way to her 'frivolous nature', running away with the dashing Lord Dalmeny and a glorious life in Europe. A few short years later and both husbands were united in grief at her graveside. It's a tale simply told, but is it as simple as that?

For those who do not know, Catherine or Katherine Canham was born at Beaumont Hall near Thorpe-le-Soken and grew into a stunning young woman. Though she had suitors, nothing came of them, and for fear of being left on the shelf at twenty-four she accepted an offer of marriage from the newly appointed vicar of Thorpe, the Revd Alexander Henry Gough. But three stormy years later, the feisty Kitty ran off to London. She changed her name and entered a second, much happier union with the son of the second Earl of Rosebury, only she forgot to mention she was already another man's wife.

Her new lifestyle could not have been more different from the old. With Lord Dalmeny she embarked upon a four-year honeymoon until, aged only thirty-two, she fell fatally ill in Verona, Italy. Confessing her bigamy on her deathbed, she asked that she be buried in Thorpe-le-Soken. Such

This is the only known likeness of Catherine 'Kitty' Canham'. The original used to hang until quite recently over the fireplace in the Bell Inn, Thorpe-le-Soken.

was her husband's devotion that he granted her wish. The ship carrying her body was bound for Harwich when it was caught in a storm and had to put in at Brightlingsea. Kitty's embalmed body was found by customs officers, but fortunately all was eventually explained – though not before Lord Dalmeny had been lodged, overnight, with his wife's body in the church on the Hythe below Colchester. Her burial at Thorpe-le-Soken was a poignant one. It is said that both husbands, in deep mourning, consoled each other by the grave in St Mary's church.

In the wake of such adventure it has been easy to sensationalise Kitty's story. She has been cast as a villain, the breaker of men's hearts, a woman prepared to replace an ageing husband in favour of a young gallant; but is that the whole story? Perhaps her craving for gaiety and pleasure was born out of loneliness despite her comfortable upbringing. Had the fact that, other than herself, no other children born to her prosperous parents lived beyond a few years unsettled her? Did the deaths of her two little brothers, Bartholomew aged four and Robert aged seven, in the same year bereave the nine-year-old Kitty enough to want to live life to the full and at all costs? Did she marry a man at odds with her own nature because she too felt that she was running out of time?

We might like to think we know the reasons why 'pretty Kitty Canham' absconded with her beau and thus into the history books, but there could be one last explanation. In the wake of a fire at The Bell Inn in Thorpe-le-Soken, and a ghostly presence in the cottage next door, perhaps the truth also lies in her three childless years with her first husband.

In an age when marriage meant almost certain pregnancy, it is strange that a young and strong woman like Kitty should not have given birth to at least one child during her three years with the Revd Gough. A man in such a revered position would surely have expected to raise a family as a result of his Christian union and may have been unable to hide his disappointment at his lack of children. Inexplicable sightings of a ghostly young woman, crying over the death of her babies by the modern day residents of Bell cottage, which at one time was part of the House Kitty shared with her first husband, could be taken to mean that Kitty conceived a child or children but they had been lost either during pregnancy or just after birth. There are no baptismal records, only a possibility that the woman's husband had blamed her for their tragedy and that she was the target of his anger.

Supernatural theories aside, there is also the possibility that if Kitty had miscarried or lost a child during a pregnancy, she may well have suffered from what is known today as post-natal depression. Deep memories of the deaths of her siblings could possibly have surfaced and with them feelings of failure, hopelessness, and fear that she could not produce a child that would live. Such feelings would have been exacerbated by any disappointment felt by her husband. Whether she was sent away to recover or fled because of her irrational fears, it was in London that she had the opportunity to meet the dashing Lord Dalmeny. Perhaps then, wishing to leave her misery behind her, she ran away with him, marrying bigamously.

There were no children either in Kitty's relationship with her new husband. Perhaps she was unable to carry a child to full term in the wake of her previous experience. Perhaps she had been left in too vulnerable a mental state to chance childbirth again. Whichever, her second marriage was happy if short-lived. At her funeral, both husbands were grief stricken, perhaps in the full knowledge of the pressure Kitty had been under in her young life.

It is perhaps pure coincidence that in a fire at the Bell Inn in 1999, everything was lost and the wall upon which a picture of Kitty Canham hung was thoroughly blackened and fire damaged. The picture itself, however, remained untouched.

LADIES OF THE DUNMOW FLITCH

He that repents him not of his marriage in a year and a day either sleeping or wakin',
May lawfully go to Dunmow and fetch a gammon of bacon.

Of all the rewards there are for marital bliss, surely the presentation of a side of bacon is the strangest? In Dunmow, since 1104 and the founding of an Augustinian Priory by Lady Juga Baynard, couples have flocked to the picturesque Essex village in the hope of qualifying for this prestigious award. The custom originates from Reginald Fitzwalter and his wife who, dressed as humble folk, begged the blessing of the Prior a year and a day after marriage. The Prior, impressed by their devotion, bestowed upon them a 'Flitch of Bacon' which prompted Fitzwalter to reveal his true identity and give some of his land to the Priory on the condition that a flitch should be awarded to any couple who could claim they were similarly devoted. Such devotion was not always easy to come by.

Not until much later in history was real importance given to the sanctity of marriage. Dynastic unions were bound by convention and of course virginity was always prized, but for the common folk in Saxon and Norman times most male–female relationships were unregulated. This casual approach to people living as man and wife (in Wessex they sold wives) gave cause for concern to clergymen. In consequence of the Church's approval of couples willing to swear an oath to the loving and stable nature of their relationship, they were happy to give an inducement to encourage their flock to provide reasonable security for their children. The pig, an invaluable commodity to any medieval husbandman, plus a significant symbol of fertility, was chosen as the most appropriate award for fidelity. Chaucer mentions the Dunmow Flitch in his *Miller's Tale*, the Wife of Bath announcing, 'The bacoun was nat fet for hem, I trowe, That som men han in Essex at Dunmowe'.

Early flitch trials awarded only the men of the relationship, seeming to ignore the women altogether. At this time the award was given purely on request; the seriousness of the oath taken was assumed to be enough to prevent fraudulent claims. The ceremony survived the Dissolution of the Monasteries, but became a civil affair conducted by the lord of the manor. By 1701, it took the form of a light-hearted manorial court complete with a 'jury' to assess the validity of the candidate's claims. At this event only ladies were asked to serve as jurors: four daughters of the lord of the manor, Elizabeth, Henrietta, Ann and Jane Beaumont, while the fifth was the daughter of his steward. Apparently this jury of single people was thought to be impartial when judging a married couple!

One Essex women who professed never to have spoken a cross word during her marriage was Anne Shakeshaft. She and her husband Thomas, a weaver from Weathersfield, were 'tried by a jury of good people' (six men and six women) in 1751 at what was to be the last public presentation of the flitch made by the lord of the manor. The event attracted 5,000 people and if Thomas had had his wits about him he would have known that such publicity would have been good for business!

Papers documenting the trial recorded that Ann and her husband had been married for more than seven years and that by reason of their quiet, peaceable, tender and loving co-habitation during all that time, they were fit and qualified to receive the bacon.

The Shakeshaft trial turned out to be an exciting and festive occasion. Lover's Knots of bright yellow silk ribbon, inscribed with 'Dunmow Bacon

The original painting of the procession of Thomas and Ann Shakeshaft winning the bacon in 1751. The painting has been copied many times. This picture was in private hands until purchased by Great Dunmow Council in 1950.

taken June 20, 1751' were worn at the presentation and in the evening everyone adjourned to the Saracens' Head, where ladies and gentlemen were dancing and playing cards. It was also a small commercial success for the couple as they made more than £10 for themselves selling slices of the bacon they had won to 'several ladies and gentlemen present' who were 'whimsically merry on the occasion'. So much was made of the event that it appeared in several printed magazines. The only regret Mrs Shakeshaft admitted to in her marriage was that she wished she had married her husband sooner.

In 1837, a flitch of bacon was presented to Mary Bloomfield and her husband Samuel, both of Great Dunmow, who was a 'labourer in husbandry'. The award cited the couple for 'highly maritorial conduct' as they had brought up a family of nine children and placed them all in respectable service without any parochial relief during a union of forty years.

Victorian trials were very well documented and named the claimants, the venue, attendance, organisers, and even the weather. They also describe how, according to the *Chelmsford Chronicle*, the ceremony on 26 July 1880 was 'farcical', that the unnamed judge was deaf and wore a high stove pipe hat and a dingy white waistcoat and cravat. The claimants, from Bethnal Green, both wore large gold earrings. The entertainment, too, was questionable, and an editorial in the newspaper remarked that the whole event had become coarse and burlesque. Even the couple's claim was dubious, but the ear-ringed gentleman was so forceful in his demands that he was awarded it by default. The newspaper also added that: 'The custom of Dunmow will hardly survive the ignominious failure of 1880.'

It did survive, taking place only on the years there were candidates willing to claim the prize. In 1912, the quaint ceremony took place, attended by 10,000 people, with only a few of that number able to observe the proceedings in the marquee erected on the flitch meadow. 'General domestic discord in the U.K.' had been cited as the reason this was the first flitch in six years. The elimination process, conducted over the previous six months, had already weeded out those who were unsuitable, including one couple, who, in claiming the bacon, had omitted to mention they were strict vegetarians.

Under the eye of the judge and in the presence of the jury, composed in accordance with tradition from young bachelors and spinsters, the proceedings began; a local newshound reported that 'a jury was assembled, one half of which would drive many a man to crime just for the sake of being tried by six girls so pretty and charmingly gowned'. With two trumpeters in scarlet uniform, a court clerk, court crier, council for claimants, and a claimant for bacon, the trial continued. The couple concerned listened as

The Dunmow flitch ceremony, around 1906.

their marriage was described as 'an Iliad in a nutshell'. Then the husband took the stand to praise the virtues of his wife of forty years. 'It's all her,' he said. 'There never was a cloud so black that she couldn't see sunshine a' back of it.' With that tribute he deferred to his wife to be questioned.

Our newshound reported that Mrs Smith was nervous as she testified as to the serenity of their lives, afraid she would say the wrong thing. As it happened there was a general consensus she really had no need to say anything. 'As the little lady stepped up on to the stand, her presence was sufficient testimony.' The report continued: 'steady eyes shone out of a calm face, framed in its bands of silvery hair. Eight children had grown to maturity in the light of those eyes and for thirty-five years she had accommodated Mr Smith's tobacco-smoking, political ways.' No wonder she deserved a side of bacon. When asked 'can you explain how you have managed to stand the vagaries of Mr Smith all these years?', she seemed not to understand. Then when asked 'in other words, how is it that you and Mr Smith have not quarreled [sic] in the past year?' she answered innocently: 'We are all the world to each other, him and me. There's been nothing to quarrel about.' Needless to say, Dunmow's historic flitch of bacon was theirs.

The Flitch Oath:

> You do swear by custom of confession
> That you ne'er made nuptual transgression

Nor since you were married man and wife
By household brawls or contentious strife
Or otherwise in bed or at board
Offended each other in deed or in word
Or in a twelve months time and a day
Repented not in thought in any way
Or since the church clerk said amen
Wish't yourselves unmarried again
But continue true and desire
As when you joined hands in holy quire.

LADY FRANCES EVELYN MAYNARD, THE SOCIALIST COUNTESS OF WARWICK (1861–1938)

I was a 'beauty' and only those who were alive then know the magic that word held for the period. I was physically fit, eighteen, unspoilt, and I adored dancing.

Frances was born the daughter of a wealthy landowner and inherited extensive family estates in 1865 following the deaths of her father and grandfather, the third Viscount Maynard. She came of age in the late nineteenth century, a time of rigid assumptions as to how ladies and gentlemen should behave. It was what set the gentry apart from the rabble, and Frances, in her elevated position, was as accepting of the status quo as the next. Men as well as women had to adhere to strict codes of conduct. They were expected to be honest, dignified, courteous, considerate and socially at ease. Men had to be disdainful of trade and money-grabbing, but should always pay gambling debts, not cheat at cards, and be honourable towards ladies. A man was not, however, bound to show the same consideration for his tradesman's debts or the reputations of female servants or village girls. The man who committed such offences was a 'cad', a 'bounder', and an 'upstart'. Gentlemanly virtues were a mark of good breeding. Lady Warwick was known to have remarked that the well bred 'have an air' while 'the middle classes may have manners but they have no manner'.

Frances herself was no shrinking violet. She rode dangerous racehorses from her stepfather's stable, went to the theatre with Disraeli, and when she discovered that she was chosen to be a possible wife of Queen Victoria's son Leopold, she emphatically declined. But she did enter the marriage market via 'the season', that elaborate ritual of 'coming out' for the daughters of the elite. This was an endless orgy of social occasions. Chaperoned dances and balls were organised by the matrons and dowagers of society and culminated in a girl's presentation at Court. As yet, English society had not been assaulted by rich American girls or 'Yankee Buccaneers' who were soon to invade England in search of a title to marry, and so Frances was unequalled in beauty and availability. She says of her introduction into society:

> I came out in the season of 1880 and my engagement to Lord Brooke was announced in June of that year. I was that rare thing, as rare as any 'oiseau bleu', a great heiresss, for America may scarcely be said as yet to have assaulted the fastness of English society. I was a 'beauty', and only those who were alive then know the magic that word held for the period. I was physically fit, eighteen, unspoilt, and I adored dancing. My stepfather and mother rented 7 Carlton Gardens for the year; the house belonged to the then Earl of Warwick, the father of the man I was destined to marry. I was married from that house. We lived there afterwards, and one of my children was born there … Many balls were given specially for me. In those days men gave balls; the Balls of the Blues and the Life Guards were noted for their excellent dancing, and the Batchelors' Ball of that season was one of the great successes … I was feasted, courted, and adored in one continual round of gaiety, and I lived in and for the moment. Nor was I a mere fool. My mentors whispered to me sometimes that my money and estates were perhaps more important than my person to some of my thronging admirers.

There followed an engagement to Lord Brook, the fifth Earl of Warwick and the 'brilliant society wedding' at Westminster Abbey in April 1881, with the Prince and Princess of Wales among the guests.

The Warwicks' aristocratic life consisted of ample leisure at their Essex home and later at Warwick castle. They were members of the Prince of Wales' Marlborough House set, and led an extravagant social life as friends of the future king. Edward had 'fast' friends and enjoyed endless rounds of gambling, horseracing, yachting, shooting, visits to the music hall, Paris, Biarritz and German spas. He preferred 'men to books and women to either'. Frances, already having provided her husband with an heir, was (as was accepted in aristocratic circles) at liberty to take a lover. It was only a matter of time – 1889 – before she became Edward's mistress.

Known by her childhood name of 'Darling Daisy', Frances was everything a socialite should be. It is said that her lover, Prince Edward, was so besotted with her that he commissioned a private railway line up to her home, Easton Lodge, and gave her an ankle bracelet inscribed 'Heaven's

Above'. Her beauty was legendary. She inspired the popular music hall ditty 'Daisy, Daisy, give me your answer, do' and habitually wore emeralds to match her eyes. Needless to say she enjoyed a long relationship with the Prince, remaining his mistress for nine years.

As with most of her 'set', Frances subscribed to the belief that 'rural society was a small select aristocracy born, booted and spurred to ride, and a large dim mass born saddled and bridled to be ridden'. But she was never unkind. Around her home at Easton Lodge, she was a common sight either out riding a 'six-in-hand, all dressed in red with a tall hat complete with a great feather', or receiving guests; she was once spotted wearing a beautiful costume of yellow muslin, covered with white lace, and a large garden hat, trimmed with roses. Once she was seen alighting from the Stortford train at Takely station, walking upon a great red carpet that had been put down for her.

'Darling Daisy' Greville. (*Author's own collection*)

Attacks on her extravagant lifestyle constantly appeared in the newspapers, but instead of angering her they triggered her social conscience. Without abandoning the position she was being ridiculed for, she used her status to promote social causes. She became a conundrum; though a countess and a landowner, she began to favour the socialist ideal of land nationalisation and pestered the Prince of Wales with her ideas for reform. Still hugely extravagant, she spent lavishly on entertaining her guests while supporting reforms to help the poor and downtrodden.

She promoted a school to encourage rural occupations at Dunmow and a scheme to train women in horticulture and agriculture. She founded a needlework school at Easton Lodge and funded a shop by which the girls could sell their work. She commissioned the famous gardener Harold Peto to landscape her gardens at the Lodge, but contracted out the labour to the Salvation Army Colony at Hadleigh, even commissioning dormitories to be built for the workforce as it was too far for them to travel to daily. So impressed was she with their hard work that she invited the men to put on their Sunday best and join her in her home for her daughter's 'coming out party' in 1903.

From these beginnings, Frances became more and more interested in the rising socialist movement. In 1904 she joined the Social Democratic Foundation and entered the world of trade unions, coal miners and railwaymen by undertaking a tour of the country. She counted among her friends fellow socialists George Bernard Shaw, H. G. Wells and Gustav Holst. Most of her old social circle had long since abandoned her. Any friendships that she could still count upon had been sorely strained when she had effectively tried to blackmail the new king, George V, with love letters she had written to his father in order to raise much needed funds.

After that scheme had failed, she wrote to help fill her ever-diminishing coffers; between 1898 and 1934 twelve books appeared under her name, the first being a book on gardens. The subjects were varied: essays on socialism; a short biography of the leader of the Arts and Crafts Movement, William Morris; a well-respected history of Warwick Castle; a book of essays on the First World War; and two substantial books of memoirs. She edited and wrote introductions or essays for a further eight books. She sailed to America in 1912 to give a lecture tour in New York and Washington while back home she contributed articles to London newspapers and the *Daily Sketch* commissioned her as an advice columnist and editor of their women's page.

Frances' charismatic character had seen her take many lovers throughout her lifetime other than Prince Edward. Her first passionate affair was with the society roué Charles Beresford, with whom she (probably) had her daughter Marjorie. But the great love of her life was millionaire bachelor

Lady Warwick's memorial is in Little Easton church, also known affectionately as the 'Maynard' church. (*Robert Hallmann*)

Joe Laycock, the faithless and callous lover who fathered two of Frances' children but broke her heart. Lord Brook, Frances' solid and dependable husband, happily gave his name to all of his wife's children (three sons and two daughters) and remained devoted to her until his death in 1924.

In 1923, Daisy Warwick stood as a candidate for the Labour Party for the parliamentary seat of Warwick and Leamington. Her opponent was her relation and later Prime Minister, Anthony Eden. But the countess, who owed money to many of those who might have supported her, was shunned and ultimately beaten into third place. Bowed but unbroken, she left parliamentary ambitions behind her, although she continued to support the Labour Party. In the late 1920s, when Frances had been a widow for some years, she tried to give her house, Easton Lodge, away first to the Labour Party and, when that failed, to the Trade Union Congress. Ironically, the fact that she was a countess and a symbol of privilege meant that her offer was rejected. Finally disillusioned with socialism, she retreated back to Easton Lodge and spent her later years concerned with the welfare of animals.

Frances, having gone from socialite to socialist, died in 1938 aged seventy-six and almost penniless. She lies buried in St Mary's church in Little Easton, which in some circles is known simply as the Maynard church. In contrast to the other grey stone tombs, her monument is a white marble bust which captures the beauty of a woman who once captured imagination of the nation and the heart of a future king.

10

LADIES OF LITERATURE, LEISURE AND LEARNING

JANE AND ANN TAYLOR,
TWINKLE TWINKLE LITTLE STAR

*T*winkle Twinkle Little Star is one of the first nursery rhymes we learn as children at our mother's knee, yet how many of us realise it was composed in Essex? Unlike other childhood favourites, such as 'Ring o' Ring o' Roses' which originated as a warning of the plague, or 'Humpty Dumpty', based on a siege engine during the Civil War, this endearing little ditty was not passed down through folklore. It was written by sisters Jane and Ann Taylor of Colchester in 1806.

The girls were born three years apart, Jane in 1783 and Ann in 1786, but Jane was a delicate child and was not expected to live through infancy. As Jane's father Isaac Taylor was an engraver and free to earn his living anywhere in the country, he moved his family to Lavenham in Suffolk, where almost immediately Jane's health improved, as did her spirit. No longer confined to a London house, Jane revelled in the simple pleasures of her parents' garden and friendly interaction of a small village. It soon became apparent to everyone who was involved with Jane that she had a natural talent for invention. As her sister in her memoirs later recalled:

> Jane was always the saucy, lively entertaining little thing – the amusement and the favourite of all that knew her. At the baker's shop she used to be placed on the kneeding-board in order to recite, preach or narrate to the great delight of his many visitors.

Jane wrote poems and plays from an early age and, though unrefined and childish, her imagination was boundless. At play she would lose herself in imaginary worlds where in happy solitude she indulged in what she called 'castle building', so much so that when she was older she cheerfully

Jane and Ann Taylor, the authors of the children's nursery rhyme *Twinkle, Twinkle Little Star*, painted by their father. (*The National Portrait Gallery*)

lamented that 'I have sometimes lived so much in a *castle*, as almost to forget that I lived in a *house*'. Later these flights of fantasy were written down.

Yet Jane was not alone in her invention. Jane's parents' house was large enough for Jane and her sister Ann to have a small room to themselves as their personal space, and here they indulged their imaginations and learnt to rely upon themselves for their own amusements. Here, and in the large garden which opened out on to distant cornfields, the sisters became close companions. They were a common sight in the village, often observed by women spinning in their doorways in the days before steam looms and factories, walking hand in hand, reciting songs and verses they had jointly composed.

Jane's talents were greatly appreciated by all that knew her, but she was a timid girl and didn't allow her head to be turned by flattery. At first, to protect their daughter's innocence, her parents kept a watchful eye on her early celebrity, but with a rapidly increasing family Jane found herself under the supervision of servants who, proud of their charge, saw no harm in letting her entertain the neighbours. When not performing, Jane would write. Examples of her writings exist from when she was about eight or nine.

In January 1796, Isaac moved his family to Colchester where he took up the position of minister of an independent congregation in the town. It was a propitious move, especially for the girls as Jane was later to describe Colchester as 'being then the station of a large body of troops, the utmost activity prevailed throughout the town; and its broad and handsome High Street was a perpetual scene of gay and busy movement.' This move marked a reduction in the family circumstances, but the house, near to the centre of the town, had a garden that Jane throughout her life referred to as the place where she was happiest.

Jane and Ann were educated at home by their father, who instilled in the girls a curiosity about every subject. At fifteen, Jane had a circle of friends who formed their own society for the reading of original essays and for the 'promotion of intellectual improvement'. She was, however, the youngest member, and with her non-competitive nature one of the more reserved of the group. Despite this, she would confidently read out her work, her essays already showing the soundness of sentiment and simplicity of style she would later be known for. Even then, and for a long time after, Jane was afraid to believe she had any talent. The meetings, however, ripened her powers of thinking and forced her to regulate her fantasies into writable material.

The first piece of Jane's writing that appeared in print was a contribution to the Minor's Pocket Book for the year 1804. Her sister had been contributing to the same publication for several years with some success and now there were those who suggested they both take on further 'literary enterprises'. Their father was proud and pleased with his daughters' accomplishments, yet did not wish them to become authors by profession. So life for the girls continued to be as dutiful as one would expect in the house of a minister, any writing by the girls snatched in quiet moments or when the day's work was done. It was under these conditions that Jane and Ann's first book *Original Poems for Infant Minds*, published in 1804, was written and found to be so 'highly agreeable to children' and so useful in their early education that it was quickly reprinted in America and translated into German and Dutch. Truly a joint production, the poems were not actually attributed to either one of the sisters exclusively. Jane, being the more timid of the sisters, would not have claimed credit for herself even if she had been asked.

Jane had written her contribution to the book while away from the parental home. Her mother's quiet but all encompassing fear of a French invasion during the autumn and winter of the year 1803 saw her send Jane, with two of her brothers and an infant sister, back to their house in Lavenham to prevent them from falling into the hands of Napoleon Bonaparte. It was not an unfounded alarm. All along the eastern coast, sea defences in the shape of Martello Towers were being built, and Colchester, as a principal military station at that time, housed a large body of troops. The public feeling was that Colchester might well be the scene of the first conflict with the invaders, and some who had the means either abandoned the city or made arrangements to be able to do so at a moment's notice. In one letter to Jane, her mother expresses her hope that 'this is not one of those awful still calms before a violent storm', noting that, 'the Butter Market is nearly walled up and made a guardhouse, and everything goes on with the utmost vicour [vigour].' In a letter from Jane to a friend, she expresses her annoyance that 'our neighbour Bonaparte should have it in his power to give us such a thorough panic'.

Jane returned to the publication of a collaborative work called *Original Poems for Infant Minds by Several Young Persons* in which contributions by herself, her sister, and others featured. It was first issued in two volumes, the first in 1804, and the second in 1805. *Rhymes for the Nursery* followed in 1806, and *Hymns for Infant Minds* in 1808. Jane began to travel to underpin her literary success, and she was well received as far away as Cornwall. An avid letter writer, she left behind her a wealth of detail about her life; one letter in particular, sent from Ilfracombe and dated 13 December 1813, shows her feelings at the impending marriage of her beloved sister Ann.

I cannot suffer this interesting morning to pass without something of a salutation from Ilfracombe; and I dare say this letter will arrive in good company; but I am sure no one will address you who can feel on this occasion either so glad, or so sorry as I do. So far as you only are concerned, I think I am entirely glad, and feel as perfectly satisfied and happy as one can do about untried circumstances. But I cannot forget that this morning which forms one indissoluble partnership, dissolves another, which we had almost considered so. I cannot – no, I cannot realize the busy scene at the Castle House, nor fancy you in your bridal appearance. I intend to place myself before the view of the house, about the time I imagine you are walking down the gravel-walk, and stand there while you are at church, and till I think you are coming back again. How strange – how sad, that I cannot be with you! What a world is this, that its brightest pleasures are, almost invariably, attended with the keenest heart-rendings ...

We have been more inseparable companions than sisters usually are; and our pursuits and interests have been the same. My thoughts of late have often wandered back to those distant years, and passed over the varied scenes which chequered our childhood and youth:–there is scarcely a recollection, in all that long period, in which we are not mutually concerned, and equally interested. If this separation had taken place ten years ago, we might, by this time, have been in some degree estranged from each other; but having passed so large and important a portion of life in such intimate union, I think we may confidently say it never will be so ...

Farewell, my dear Ann! and in this emphatical farewell, I would comprehend all the wishes, the prayers, the love, the joy, and the sorrow, which it would be so difficult to express in more words. If there is a dash of bitterness in the grief with which I bid you farewell, it is only from the recollection that I have not been to you the sister I might have been.

Jane produced several solitary works including *Essays in Rhyme on Morals and Manners*, finished in the spring of 1816. In later years her brother wrote that 'she had never wrote any thing with so much zest and excitement, as the pieces composing this volume. While employed upon them, she was almost lost to other interests – even her prevailing domestic tastes seemed forgotten; and in our daily walks, she was often quite abstracted from the scene around her.'

In 1817, Jane wrote *Correspondence between a Mother and Her Daughter at School* in collaboration with her mother. By now she had developed a way of working that saw her only write in the mornings. This was only after a walk or a ramble after breakfast, and then armed with ideas and an excitement she would return to write them down. She never had a precise plan but worked 'in a fever' for two or three hours after which she would go for a second walk, only rarely writing again in the afternoon.

By 1819, Jane's health had begun to deteriorate and she suffered from a chronic breathlessness, which she described as 'an inward tempest'. After a long illness attributed to cancer she died in April 1824, aged only forty-one. She was laid to rest in the burial ground of the meeting house at Ongar, where a simple monument has been erected to mark the spot. Jane's sister Ann outlived her, dying herself in 1866. The National Trust has a permanent exhibition (including paintings, books and personal belongings) on the Taylor family in the Lavenham Guildhall.

Twinkle, Twinkle Little Star was written in 1806 and consists of five verses:

> Twinkle, twinkle, little star,
> How I wonder what you are!
> Up above the world so high,
> Like a diamond in the sky.
> Twinkle, twinkle, little star,
> How I wonder what you are!
>
> When the blazing sun is gone,
> When he nothing shines upon,
> Then you show your little light,
> Twinkle, twinkle, all the night.
> Twinkle, twinkle, little star,
> How I wonder what you are!
>
> Then the traveller in the dark,
> Thanks you for your tiny spark,
> He could not see which way to go,
> If you did not twinkle so.
> Twinkle, twinkle, little star,
> How I wonder what you are!
>
> In the dark blue sky you keep,
> And often through my curtains peep,
> For you never shut your eye,
> Till the sun is in the sky.
> Twinkle, twinkle, little star,
> How I wonder what you are!

As your bright and tiny spark,
Lights the traveller in the dark,–
Though I know not what you are,
Twinkle, twinkle, little star.
Twinkle, twinkle, little star,
How I wonder what you are!

CLARISSA TRANT, ESSEX DIARIST (1800–1844)

Oh, for a few mountains or even hills in Essex ...

Women, if they were literate, have always 'written'. Their letters, diaries, journals and essays have shown us the minutiae of their everyday lives. How else was a woman to express herself? With men running their lives, at least a woman's thoughts and feelings were her own and free to be set down on paper. From the medieval *Paxton Letters*, detailing a mother's concerns for her family, to the detailed written accounts of genteel Victorian ladies while undertaking the 'Grand Tour' of Europe, a woman's correspondence was a vital means of expression. Clarissa Trant is a perfect example of a female writer. Her diary in twenty-eight volumes is a wonderful picture of how women of her time thought and talked, her unusual upbringing giving her a wider experience of life than most of her peers. It was eventually published by her granddaughter in 1925.

It's a wonder Clarissa was able to settle in Essex after the life she had led as the daughter of a distinguished but impoverished Irish army officer. As a consequence of his service abroad, the Trants had lived in England, Ireland, and on the continent, often staying with wealthy friends and relations, but sometimes living in humble circumstances and meeting some extraordinarily characters. As a young child, Clarissa saw Napoleon ride through the streets of Boulogne when all other English families had been ordered out of town. For a while the family had been indulged by the French mayor, but eventually they had to go to Valenciennes, transported together with 1,500 other British subjects as Bonaparte's 'hostages for the good conduct of the English Government'. Boulogne was also where Clarissa's sister was born and died after a few weeks. Luckily, via a certain Lady Tweedale, the family obtained a passport and returned to England.

Clarissa's parents were devoted to each other, but her mother was a fragile woman. By 1805, the protracted separations from her husband during army campaigns in Egypt had taken their toll on her health and she was diagnosed with dropsy. She died in 1806 and Clarissa never forgot her 'pale face and gentle smile'. Clarissa too had dubious health; while

Clarissa Trant, the daughter of a well-travelled and distinguished army officer,
settled happily in Essex when she became the wife of the Reverend John Bramston.
Her diaries in twenty-eight volumes give us a unique insight into a nineteenth-
century woman's life. (*Essex Record Office*)

her father was away on a special mission to Portugal, Clarissa attended numerous schools with numerous nurses for the benefit of her health. Her father, aware of having lost his wife, was always anxious for Clarissa and, as a result, their relationship was close, though she often thought that he loved her more than she deserved. When at school she thought the others pupils to be as 'as spoiled and disagreeable as myself', and reminded her friends constantly how thankful they should always be for a mother's care.

By 1811, it was safe for Clarissa to join her father in Oporto. By now, for his services to England he had been appointed to Brigadier General by Sir Arthur Wellesley, the Duke of Wellington, whom Clarissa met on many occasions and featured in her diaries. As soon as she was able, she and her brother travelled to Portugal on a Lisbon packet to meet their father after many years.

Clarissa grew to be intelligent, witty, kind, and very attractive. Her mind was as nimble as her pen, and her journals suggest she had at least twelve suitors, despite her lack of fortune. Though well travelled, (she undertook grand tours of Switzerland, Germany, Italy, and Rome) she did not associate with the highest society, but could count among her friends great names of the period such as Lord John Russell; the Prince of Orange; Talleyrand; Sir Charles Stuart; George Canning; the Duke of Wellington; and Daniel O'Connell. On 19 October 1828, Clarissa wrote in her diary: 'I never spent a pleasenter [sic] day on board a stem [sic] packet thanks to our encounter with a most agreeable and well informed and at the same time truly religious young clergyman, a J. Bramston, who has been in Rome when we were there.' At the age of thirty-one, Clarissa was finding herself quite taken with the spiritually compatible clergyman who was vicar of Great Baddow, Essex. Though her affections had been roused by the ardent attentions of a Colonel Cameron in her younger days, his parents had queried his choice and he had not fought for her. Now she felt that Bramston's sober wooing was right for her, and they married, after a suitable engagement, in 1832.

Her marriage to the serious Reverend John Bramston was a happy one, even though the life of a country parson was at serious odds with her former adventures, and she longed for a hill or two amongst the endless Essex pastures. But she was glad of a permanent place at last and made friends with her husband's family, often staying at Hallingbury Park, the residence of Mary Archer Houblon (John's Aunt), and Willingdale Doe vicarage, the family home, as well as visiting her friends the Rayleighs at Terling.

Her greatest regret was that she could not help her husband with his duties as her 'wretched health' was a handicap. She wrote in her diaries of the 'stress and strain' of her youth, when 'both my head and my heart were overworked', and wrote constantly of all the pleasures her relationship brought her: the peace of her married life, her three children, Clara, Mary and John, and her 'delicious' home.

One of her greatest sorrows was the death of her brother Tom at Great Baddow. He had died soon after she married, and her father, who had subsequently resettled nearer to his daughter, had followed in 1839. Clarissa continued to suffer from persistent ill health, and at times her memory suffered and she became distressed that she too did not have long to live. In 1840 her husband became the vicar of Witham and for a while the change seemed to benefit Clarissa, but four years later, on 10 April 1844, she died there of 'pleurisy with complications'. She is buried in St Nicholas' churchyard.

SARAH FULLER FLOWER (1805–1848)

Tall, singularly beautiful, with noble and regular features; in manner she was gay and impulsive, her conversation full of sparkling wit and kindly humour.

(Mrs Bridell-Fox, kinswoman to the Flower family)

What do the fateful sinking of a White Star Liner, a courageous orchestra, and the daughter of Benjamin Flower have to do with Essex? A simple hymn is the answer. It was heard by those in the lifeboats as the *Titanic* went down in the early hours of 15 April 1912, played by those and for those who knew they were about to slip into the icy depths of the Atlantic. The hymn was 'Nearer, my God, to Thee', published in 1841 and composed by Sarah Fuller Flower of Harlow, Essex. The song may have been immortalised for its part in the most tragic maritime disaster in English history, but Sarah is still widely unknown. Out of the millions of people today who raise their voices to this brief lyrical poem of adoration, there are comparatively few who have any idea who the author was.

Sarah Fuller Flower was born in 1805 at Harlow, the youngest daughter of a couple who met for the first time in Newgate Prison. Her father, Benjamin Flower was the son of a London tradesman. After a time abroad, he returned to England as editor and political writer of a pro-revolutionary journal called the *Cambridge Intelligencer* (to which the poet Coleridge, among others, contributed). But his opposition to war with France got him into trouble with the law, saw him tried at the bar of the House of Lords, and imprisoned for six months. Sarah's mother, Elizabeth Gould, became a regular visitor to Newgate and after a warm relationship had

Sarah Fuller Flower from Harlow was the writer of the hymn 'Nearer, my God, to Thee', published in 1841. This beautiful hymn was chosen to be played by the orchestra aboard the ill-fated *Titanic* in the early hours of 15 April 1912 in an attempt to comfort those who knew they were about to slip into the icy depths of the Atlantic.

developed into love, she and Benjamin married upon his release and settled in Harlow.

Two daughters followed: Elizabeth in 1803 and Sarah eighteen months later. Both girls were talented. Elizabeth showed a remarkable gift for music while Sarah wrote charming poetry, including the hymn in question, prompting the eminent nineteenth-century poet and essayist James Henry Leigh-Hunt to describe her as 'a rare mistress of thoughts and tears'. Sadly, in 1810, the girls lost their mother and were thereafter raised by their father until he too died in 1829. Both girls then came under the care of

Revd William Johnson Fox, a Unitarian minister, and before long Sarah was in charge of musical arrangements at the minister's chapel.

Sarah's poetry was not conventionally or solemnly composed. Rather, her impulsive and exhilarating personality was they key to every line she wrote. 'They were the unforced utterances of some insistent and powerful emotion,' commented Mrs Bridell-Fox, who believed it was the beauty of the Essex countryside that inspired Sarah's 'strong impulse and feeling of the moment'. Her hymns at the time were applauded in *The Times* and are known to have given American president William McKinley, when near to death, tremendous consolation. The attending physician reported that among McKinley's last words were '"Nearer, my God, to Thee, / E'en though it be a cross" has been my constant prayer.' On the afternoon of 13 September 1901, after five minutes of silence across America, bands in Union and Madison Squares in New York City played the hymn in honour of the fallen president. The sincere and sacred song was also played at a memorial service for him in Westminster Abbey.

As a young woman, Sarah could count Robert Browning among her friends, and she assisted in the publication of the poet's first book. There were also rumours that had she not been romantically involved elsewhere, Browning would have chosen Sarah's exciting personality to focus his thoughts upon. Sarah, however, became the wife of a scientific engineer named William Adams, and went to live with her husband in London, which she loved for its history and architecture.

Sadly, Sarah Adams, as she had become, was to die relatively young at the age of forty-three on 14 August 1848. Her beloved sister had died of consumption only two years before. With such a short moment in the spotlight for the Flower sisters, it was fortunate that their lifelong companion, Mrs Bridell-Fox, preserved all the sisters' compositions and donated them to the British Museum. 'Nearer, my God, to Thee', as well as being forever linked to the *Titanic* disaster, was also said to have been a favourite hymn of King Edward VII.

11

ESSEX GIRLS IN FICTION

MOLL FLANDERS

The Fortunes and Misfortunes of the Famous Moll Flanders, Etc. Who Was Born In Newgate, and During a Life of Continu'd Variety For Threescore Years, Besides Her Childhood, Was Twelve Year a Whore, Five Times a Wife [Whereof Once To Her Own Brother], Twelve Year a Thief, Eight Year a Transported Felon In Virginia, At Last Grew Rich, Liv'd Honest, and Died a Penitent. Written from her own Memorandums.

With a title as long as this, it's a wonder there was any need for Daniel Defoe to write the story of this Essex girl at all. Luckily it is better known simply as *Moll Flanders* and was published in 1722, three years after Defoe's success with *Robinson Crusoe*.

Defoe has Moll born in Newgate, but places her firmly in Colchester from the age of nine and throughout her formative years. Having been a pamphleteer and journalist before he became a novelist, Defoe had difficulty omitting social comment from his work and had placed Moll in this corner of Essex deliberately. He knew Colchester well from many visits and he had purchased several hundred acres of land in the area, with a view to setting up a tile factory. He was also aware that Colchester had a thinly veiled and grisly reputation for illegitimacy and 'infanticide'. In *Moll*, he sought to publicise the plight of desperate women and promote the need for 'foundling hospitals', something he was passionate about in his days as a journalist.

For those who are not acquainted with our heroine, Moll is herself illegitimate and in the course of trying to better herself she has illegitimate children of her own. Defoe makes his heroine's life a complex tale, but gives her the advantage of straightforward thinking, then considered to be a typically masculine character trait, which proves to be her salvation. As

The old and the new meet at North Bridge in Colchester. Moll Flanders would have
been familiar with cottages such as these as she grew to womanhood in Essex's
oldest town. Although Defoe did not have his heroine dispose of her illegitimate
child in such a manner, Colchester in the late seventeenth and early eighteenth
centuries was the location of multiple infanticide cases. In the 1630s, one inhabitant
'buried one child, poisoned another and smothered a third', all illegitimate. It was
not unusual to see the bodies of drowned children floating in the river or to come
across infants left in doorways. (*Robert Bowman*)

if to remind women that there is a penalty to be paid for having a restless
spirit, Moll's character finds herself in the predicament women have found
themselves in since time immemorial. Unlike today, bastardy was the sole
responsibility of the mother and legislation was in place to hinder, not help,
the woman in question. Laws existed to punish the offender and sentence
her to time in a House of Correction. The notorious 'Fornication' Act of
1624 had made adultery and incest a capital offence, and the combination
of these constraints prompted many women to hide their pregnancies and
rid themselves of the child once it was born. Consequently, infanticide had
become 'a pest to the public', but few cases were ever proven in court. At
the time Defoe created Moll Flanders, infanticide was something neither
the Church nor the state could properly prevent or punish.

Colchester in the late seventeenth and early eighteenth centuries was
the location of multiple infanticide cases. In an incident in the 1630s, one
inhabitant 'buried one child, poisoned another, and smothered a third',
all illegitimate. It was not unusual to see the bodies of drowned children
floating in rivers, or come across infants left in doorways. By virtue of

her birth, Moll Flanders had associated all her life with women desperate enough to dispose of their children in such ways. She, however, was not. For Moll has always known of 'Mother Midnight', a network of wet nurses and midwives, who for a sum levelled at the amount a woman could pay would take away an unwanted infant and 'dispose' of it for the mother.

At a time when the 'foundling' lobbyists were trying to establish a network of help for such mothers, this underground organization already existed as part of a black economy. What happened to the individual children taken by these women was never known to the mother. Chances are for another fee – at the receiving end – they were adopted by childless couples or reared as part of an underclass until old enough to be sold into work. What mattered was that the mothers who gave up their babies could always tell themselves their child was enjoying a future she herself could never provide.

Defoe made his heroine independent, intelligent and resilient, traits not recognised as desirable in an eighteenth-century Essex woman, or any woman for that matter. Less desirable was the Colchester backdrop against which Moll played out her early life. But in 1739, the first foundling hospital was established in London 'for the education and maintenance of exposed and deserted young children'. Perhaps Defoe had made his point at last.

THE

FORTUNES

AND

MISFORTUNES

Of the FAMOUS

Moll Flanders, &c.

Who was Born in NEWGATE, and during a Life of continu'd Variety for Threescore Years, besides her Childhood, was Twelve Year a *Whore*, five times a *Wife* (whereof once to her own Brother) Twelve Year a *Thief*, Eight Year a Transported *Felon* in *Virginia*, at last grew *Rich*, liv'd *Honest*, and died a *Penitent*,

Written from her own MEMORANDUMS.

LONDON: Printed for, and Sold by W. CHETWOOD, at *Cato's-Head*, in *Russel-street, Covent-Garden*; and T. EDLING, at the *Prince's-Arms*, over-against *Exeter-Change* in the *Strand*. MDDCXXI.

Title page of Daniel Defoe's
Moll Flanders, 1722.

MEHALAH

I will marry you and take your name, but only to save mine. That is all.
I will neither love you, nor live with you save as I do now. These are my
terms. If you will take them, so be it. If not we shall go on as before.

Her name was Mehalah but she was known as 'Glory'. Immediately there is a sense of bounty about this Essex Girl – a fierce independence. She has gypsy blood in her veins, yet is loyal and true. Both wild and resourceful, she is Essex personified, unaware of her beauty, but beautiful just the same.

Her creator, the Reverend Sabine Baring-Gould, spent ten years from 1871 as minister for East Mersea and is perhaps better known for having penned that favourite among hymns, 'Onward Christian Soldiers'. When he arrived to take up his ministry, he was a man of thirty-seven with a young wife and eleven-month-old daughter. When he died in 1924, he was weeks short of his ninetieth birthday, having fathered fourteen children and written prolifically. *Mehalah* was his first novel, the inspiration for which he drew from his remote surroundings. Characters were based on his neighbours and placed in locations that were on his doorstep.

In melodramatic Victorian language, he describes the desolation of the region cut off at high tide, 'leaving standing out of the flood only the long island of Mersea and the lesser islet, called the Ray'. He describes how the Ray is not approachable by road 'unless the sun or east wind has parched the ooze into brick and then the way is long and tortuous among bitter pools and shining creeks'. But his wordy prose reaches its apogee when he describes how in summer 'the thrift mantles the marshes with shot satin, passing through all graduations of tint from maiden's blush to lily white ... thereafter a purple glow steals over the waste, as sea lavender bursts into flower and simultaneously every creek and pool is royally fringed with sea aster.'

A place of such sharp contrasts was bound to produce a character such as Mehalah, whether in fiction or fact. She is essentially her own woman. Free thinking and untameable, she has a will of her own. Her heart belongs to whom she chooses and no man shall have it by force. Though she rows her own boat, carries a pistol and wears the scarlet woven cap of a boatman (the bonnet rouge of the French Revolution), she is more a woman for it. Her scarlet kerchief and navy blue jersey is a far cry from the restrictive corsets of the Victorian dame, and reveals more about her as a person than it conceals.

She is more than a match for her suitor, Elijah Rebow, a relentless bully who will stop at nothing to possess her and makes it quite clear that it

All that remains of the 'little hunch-backed church at Virley', where Mehalah married Elijah Rebow. In the absence of a proper wedding band, a link of chain was used: 'we shall use a ring such as has never been used before, because our union is unlike all other unions,' Renbow declared placing the ring on Mehalah's finger. 'Our bond, Glory,' he added, in a low tone, 'is not of gold, but of iron.' The church fell in the Great Essex Earthquake of 1884. (*Robert Hallmann*)

is not a 'match' or equal that he wants in Mehalah. In one encounter, tortured by her disregard for him, Rebow restrains her, demanding: 'Listen to me, Glory, you must and shall. You do not love me, Glory, because you do not fear me. A woman will never love her equal, but she will worship her superior.' As if to press home his point he continues: 'I am no more to be escaped from than fate. I am mighty over you as providence!'

It is this battle of wills that drives the novel. That, plus Rebow's relentless pursuit, his puritanical rhetoric, the unforgiving landscape, and Mehalah's pride. It is also Baring-Gould's observations of other Essex women complete with their idiosyncrasies. In direct contrast to the heroine, there is the petty-minded coquette, Phoebe Mussett, and the glorious Mrs De Witt dressed out in her military coat of scarlet 'bought second hand at Colchester'.

Gould based Mrs De Witt upon the wife of William Baker, a mariner, who lived in an old hulk anchored high up on the shingle of the 'hard'. Both he and his wife in turn would row those that had business in Brightlingsea across the estuary at low tide and then 'pick-a-back' them through the mud. Baker himself was a sober man but his wife was fond of a little refreshment, and when one night she returned from a ferrying 'overcome with liquor', Baker had already hauled up the ladder. As she called to be admitted on to the boat, Baker doused her with water from a pail, leaving her to 'swear, scold and shiver' until he thought she was fit to be let on board.

Both Mehalah and Mrs De Witt can be found in the Mersea census of that period – that is to say the women who inspired Baring-Gould. It was

Mr and Mrs Baker, who lived on an old barge at East Mersea, featured as characters in *Mehalah*. They are aboard their barge *Pandora*, tied up at East Mersea in 1894. The two sailor boys were summer visitors.

thought that Mehalah was Mr Baker's daughter from a previous marriage to a woman called Hannah by whom he also had a son, William. The second Mrs Baker pictured with her husband in 1894 with their barge *Pandora* was often called 'matey' by William, but her real name was Ann.

If Mehalah Baker was indeed the girl behind our eponymous heroine, she was thirteen years old when Sabine Baring-Gould first became Mersea's minister. She worked as servant to Customs Officer James Rodger and his family who lived in Brightlingsea High Street. She does not appear in the 1881 census. Rumour has it that she ran away with a young soldier of the name Gardiner or Gardener from Colchester barracks. And so, there may be more to an Essex girl on the page than at first we thought.

BIBLIOGRAPHY

Arnold, J., *Queen Elizabeth's Wardrobe Unlock'd* (1988).

Baring-Gould, S., *Mehalah: A Story of the Salt Marshes* (1880).

Barnes, T. L., *A Nun's Life: Barking Abbey in the Late-Medieval and Early Modern Periods* (2004).

Beckett, R. A., *Romantic Essex: Pedestrian Impressions* (1907).

Bentley, R., *Excerpts from the Letters of Horace Walpole, Earl of Orford, v.4 1759-1764* (1840).

Bremer, F., *John Winthrop: America's Forgotten Founding Father* (2003).

Carlton, C., *Charles I: The Personal Monarch* (1995).

Clifton, K. A. (ed.), *Memorials of Old Essex* (1908).

Dale, S., *The History and Antiquities of Harwich and Dovercourt, in the County of Essex* (1732).

Dovey, Z., *An Elizabethan Progress* (1996).

Emmison, F. G., *Elizabethan Life: Morals & the Church Courts* (1973).

Emmison, F. G., *Tudor Food and Pastimes: Life at Ingatestone Hall* (1964).

Freedman, S., *Poor Penelope: Lady Penelope Rich, An Elizabethan Woman* (1983).

Hallmann, R., *Essex History You Can See* (2006).

Hankins, J. R., *Local Government and Society in Early Modern England: Hertfordshire and Essex. 1590–1630* (1975).

Harrison, J. F., *Late Victorian Britain 1875-1901* (1991).

Hope, T. M. (ed.), 'Amazons at Brentwood', *Essex Pie* (1952).

Macfarlane, A., *Witchcraft in Tudor and Stuart England* (1970).

Murphy, B. A., *Bastard Prince* (2001).

Neale, K., *Essex in History* (1997).

Osborne, J., *Entertaining Elizabeth I, the Progresses and Great Houses of her Time* (1989).

Petchey, W. J., *A Prospect of Maldon, 1500-1689* (1991).

Pollock, L., *With Faith and Physic: The Life of a Tudor Gentlewoman – Lady Grace Mildmay, 1552–1620* (1993).

Radune, R., *Pequot Plantation: The Story of an Early Colonial Settlement* (2005).

Roberts, C., *Founding Mothers: The Women Who Raised Our Nation* (2004).

Skidmore, G. (ed.), *Elizabeth Fry: A Quaker Life: Selected Letters & Writings* (2005).

St John Mildmay, Lt-Col. H. A., *A Brief Memoir of the Mildmay Family* (1913).

Steer, F. W., *The History of the Dunmow Flitch Ceremony* (1951).

Taylor, J., *Memoirs, Correspondence, and Poetical Remains* (1832).

Walter J., and Wrightson, K., 'Dearth and the Social Order in Early Modern England', *Past and Present*, 1976.

Wilson, V. A., *Society Women of Shakespeare's Time* (1924).

Zunshine, L., *Bastards and Foundlings: Illegitimacy in Eighteenth-Century England* (2005).

INDEX